# THE POWER

## OF YOUR

# SUPERMIND

## Vernon Howard

**New Life Foundation**
**www.anewlife.org**

*For details on other Vernon Howard books, CDs, DVDs,
MP3 CDs, classes and much more contact us at:*

**NEW LIFE FOUNDATION
PO Box 2230
Pine, Arizona 85544
(928) 476-3224**

**Web: www.anewlife.org
E-mail: info@anewlife.org**

ISBN 1-934162-50-7

LIBRARY OF CONGRESS
CATALOG CARD NUMBER 75024047

# *Notes*

# How This Book Can Work For You

Imagine an artist in a colorful meadow, happily painting. He is in a sunny spot. But later, the sun changes its position, leaving him in shadows. While preferring sunshine, he takes no action to change himself, and so remains in shadows.

Finally, he gets tired of the dark place. So, by personal effort, he moves himself in relation to the sun. Once more he feels the sunshine's warm cheer. Also, he paints expertly with ease and enjoyment.

You can be the psychic artist who moves over to eternal sunshine. This book, the *Supermind*, provides that guidance. It is for those who honestly feel they have not as yet stepped over to the true brightness of understanding and action, but would like to do so. The *Supermind* provides *esoteric* wisdom. This means that you will meet many answers which at first seem strange. But wondrously, as you earnestly persist, strangeness is replaced by new insight. This new *psychic sight* changes and uplifts everything for you not previously thought possible.

This great change is much more than the addition of intellectual knowledge. It is something you can feel personally, definitely and clearly. You *sense a difference,* just as you might feel the difference in weight between a pencil and a book.

What can *Supermind* do for you? You will discover:

1. *Answers to baffling questions you have asked for years, such as the meaning and purpose of life on earth, and what to do for true success.*

2. *Inspiring techniques for sensible and carefree living in a world which knows little of them.*

3. *How great Cosmic wisdoms can be explained in a clear and practical way.*

4. *How to be free of the need to make painful or nerve-wracking decisions, which usually turn out to be wrong.*

5. *How psychic health provides new and refreshing solutions to physical problems, like sleeplessness and nervousness, etc.*

6. *Why things happen as they do, and the secret for benefiting from whatever happens.*

7. *How to awaken fresh energies that carry you effortlessly forward to true riches.*

Give the principles of *Supermind* your special and faithful attention for the first three weeks. Review and ponder. Give its esoteric ideas time to work for you.

When printed it italics, the word *Supermind* refers to this book; otherwise, it means the Mind itself.

Included throughout the book are series of questions and answers, typical of those discussed in my lectures and classes. They can nourish your understanding and usage of the power of your Supermind in a very special way.

Read this book in an easy manner, with relaxed enjoyment, just as if we were talking things over in your home. In one sense, that is what we are doing.

Our aim is to make grand discoveries and how to use them for a glorious, new, satisfying life. It can be done by you as it has been done by others through *Supermind*.

— *Vernon Howard*

# CONTENTS

# Notes

# 1

# The Marvelous Powers of Your Supermind

Once upon a time a community of eagles lived on a beautiful mountain range. They were carefree and happy, finding an abundance of natural foods in the surrounding woods and streams. Their days were spent in lofty soaring and peaceful pleasure.

But down on the dry prairie there dwelled a band of clever crows. Merchants by occupation, the crows had invested their money in growing a low grade of corn. Looking around for potential customers, they spotted the high-flying eagles. "Sell them corn" was the battle-cry of the crows as they plotted their persuasions.

"Wrap the corn in a glittering package," suggested one crow. "Get the eagles dependent upon us," advised another. "Most important of all," counseled one crow with considerable success in selling corn, "convince the eagles that our corn is not merely a need, but an absolute must. Persuade them that without it they will be lonely, loveless, lost. A good starting place is to load them with a false sense of guilt. Just make them feel guilty over ignoring our corn — and we've got them!"

Now, the eagles were intelligent enough, but somewhat careless in their thinking. Though they were cautious at first, the corn looked pretty good. Besides, it saved the effort of hunting around on their own.

So the eagles soared less and less and dropped down to the cornfields more and more. Of course, the less they flew, the less they felt like flying. Growing weak in their wings, they had to hop awkwardly over the ground. This led to frequent collisions with each other, followed by quarrels.

But there was one eagle whose eyesight also gave him insight. He sensed something very wrong about the whole operation. Besides, *the corn just didn't taste right.* When he tried to persuade his friends to return to the mountains, the crows ridiculed him as a troublemaker. Believing the crows, the eagles shunned their former friend.

So the more corn the crows peddled, the more corn the eagles swallowed. But something had now happened to the once lofty kings of birds. They complained a lot. They were nervous and irritable. They felt lonely, loveless, lost. Every once in awhile they would remember their mountain home, but couldn't remember the way back. And so they sullenly existed, hoping for something better to turn up, which never did.

Growing tired of it all, the keen-eyed eagle studied himself carefully. Discovering his wings, he tried them out. They worked! So off he flew, back to the mountains. From dawn to sunset, he soared over his world, carefree and happy.

And this is how any man, tired of it all, can fly up and away to his natural freedom and happiness.

And this is what *Supermind* is all about.

## The Exalted State of the Amazing Supermind

Since it is necessary to select a single word to indicate the Higher Force covered in this book, I choose to call it the Supermind.

The definition of Supermind is not complex; it is quite

simple. I mean the mental faculty which is above and beyond conditioned human thought. It is the same thing as *awareness, consciousness, esoteric thinking.* It is what an Eastern mystic would call the *silent mind,* or what the New Testament calls the *Kingdom of Heaven* within. It is your *true self.* Quite simply, it is the force within every man that is as high above the ordinary mind as the sky is above earth.

The state of the Supermind cannot be described with words; it must be experienced by the individual seeker. It is best explained by what it is *not.* It is definitely not the conditioned mind. The Supermind is free of all negative conditioning. It has no fear, no painful cravings, no doubts. It knows everything needed to be known for a successful life and it is happy. The conditioned mind is that part of us which has been influenced and molded since birth. It is an acquired mass of opinions, beliefs, contradictions, and mechanical reactions, all of which get us into trouble. The conditioned mind does not represent a man's basic self; therefore, *man can and must break away from it.*

Our everyday mind can start the search for the new life, but sooner or later we must rise above it to Supermind.

We now come to what is perhaps the trickiest trap set in the path of the spiritual pilgrim — his blithe assumption that he can use *conditioned* thinking to find truth and reality. *Impossible!* The everyday mind, although conditioned, is strictly limited in its activities, like a collie dog tied to a post.

The ordinary mind consists of stored up memories of facts. It knows only the old, habitual ways. Now, this is good and necessary whenever we want to conduct our business or cook a dinner for we call upon our memory of facts.

But any attempt to use the mechanical mind to penetrate the spiritual world will always fail, even if it appears to itself to succeed. Genuine spirituality means to break into the unknown, the unconditioned. And this is why so many seekers fail. They inwardly or fearfully resist the unknown

14

mysteries of reality or they prefer the falsely assumed security of familiar words and exterior authorities.

To repeat, the Supermind has nothing to do with the storing up of memorized ideas, including those of spiritual matters. If we are wrong about spiritual matters and have a dozen college degrees, we are still wrong.

This brings us to a vital principle: We must not make imaginative assumptions as to the nature of the Supermind. Such assumptions will spring from the *old* mind and will produce another *old* picture, although perhaps in a different kind of frame. We must guard against seeing what we merely wish to see.

Assume nothing whatsoever about the Supermind, any more than you would assume the nature of a countryside you intend to visit. You would not tell the countryside what it should be like; you would let it surprise you with its newness. Do likewise with Supermind!

Supermind exists within everyone, but man is asleep to it. Our entire task on earth is to awaken to the unfoldments of Supermind.

## The Practical Power of Supermind

Is this esoteric knowledge of the Supermind practical for modern man? If the world could only see it, it is the *only* force capable of clearing the human jungle of endless frustrations. Man has tried everything — science, psychology, social schemes, peace conferences, moral systems, religions, philosophies — and chaos continues. Man has failed because he has not sincerely tried the way of esoteric knowledge. But the individual man or woman who wants peace for himself or herself in a warring world can try it with success.

To determine if it is practical, let us examine the following:

One of the first results of psychic upliftment is that unwanted events cease to happen. Why? Because exterior conditions spring from our inner states. So as we raise our level, exterior problems fall away. We are no longer their victims. To be in charge of an exterior situation means one thing and one thing only — to be in charge of your inner self.

Fear cannot exist for the man who has risen from his ordinary mind to Supermind. It is as if a child ran toward home at night after mistaking a swaying tree for a hovering ghost. If he were able to dismiss his fearful imagination, he would see the tree as a tree and stop running. When we see false appearances as false, we are at home wherever we are, because we are not afraid. *He who has found the bliss of the Eternal has no fear from any quarter. (Taittiriya Upanishad)*

It is both startling and delightful to discover that another world exists far above our petty desires and demands. Then comes the great relief long sought, for everyone somehow suspects that his basic problem is the kind of mental world he inhabits. We used to think that the problem was the harsh world other people handed us. But, we awakened. We saw that our own attitudes created the harsh world. With that insight came new strength to destroy the old world. Upon its destruction we built the new.

Don't be afraid to play through life. Retire from heavy thoughts. Take everything with lighthearted wisdom. We are heavy because we think we must make an impression, gain something, be somebody. In spite of what society tells you, you need not be anybody at all in the eyes of men. The only genuine need you have is to be a real human being. Try to see this, try to feel it with all your heart. Then you will know what it means to make the world your plaything.

Is esoteric knowledge practical? We see that it is so when we first detect the utterly impractical ideas of the habitual mind.

Imagine yourself approaching the border of a country you are eager to visit. But upon reaching the border, you are blocked. There is a pole across the road, guards demand your passport, various rules bar your entrance.

What ruins your journey? Man-made regulations and

boundaries of the political world. But there are no such barriers to your entrance into the nation of the inner self. Bars *seem* to be there, but none exist. Man-made ideas and restrictions which we adopted while unaware can be dropped. By realizing this, anyone can enter the wondrously new nation within himself.

## You Live in Two Worlds at the Same Time

You really live in two different worlds at the same time! We will refer to them in this book as the Inner World and the Outer World. The understanding of this does much to clear away confusion and to add psychic and cosmic strength to you.

You live in the Outer World of the physical body, other people, homes, finances, government, travel, automobiles and so on. You also dwell in the Inner World of your thoughts, feelings, desires, insight, curiosity and other psychological items. You must place your Inner World first in your order of thinking. This is a primary teaching of every *true* religion and philosophy, including those discussed in this book.

Why must the inner, spiritual kingdom come *first?* Because the *inner controls and determines the outer.* It is just as simple as that. However, the mass of mankind, while giving lip service to this truth, does not actually realize it, which accounts for the neuroses of the masses.

Let's see how this connects with your future: It is right and necessary to plan ahead in exterior affairs, such as a future home. It is not right to insistently plan how and where you will be happy tomorrow. For one thing, the future will not bend to our demands. But, most important is that *thinking of something in tomorrow which will make us happy is to postpone the enjoyment possible in today.*

The more you live from your psychic world, the easier becomes your real living of life. Instead of fumbling with financial problems, demands of society upon you, and with

17

your own confusions, you know exactly what to do. And one thing you do is to *cease to be anxious* toward them.

Take the painful problem of making daily decisions. Let's see how an understanding of your "two worlds" abolishes this torment for you.

On the physical plane, it is necessary to make decisions, but these need not bother us. We can follow the desire of the moment in selecting the blue suit rather than the black one, or take tea instead of coffee.

*No decisions are necessary when living from the high level of the Supermind.* When we have abolished the false self, which consists of contradictory desires, we need make no choice at all in matters pertaining to contentment. There are no opposing forces, therefore, nothing to choose. We just live triumphantly according to the principles of Supermind.

When we are in the right stream, we have no concern with the movements of the boat from left to right; that is, we need not care what life decides for us. *We just let it decide and happily enjoy the ride.* This idea of flowing along with life, and not interfering with its natural process, is a valuable contribution of Taoism.

Realize that you live in these two worlds simultaneously. Again and again place the Inner World first. You will be at home in both worlds. As you read along you may ask, "Yes, this is a fascinating search, but what should I *do?* I need to know exactly what to do and how to do it." Remember, everything you read tells you what to do, even though its newness makes it seem strange. It is like temporarily fumbling to open an envelope containing a map to a fabulous treasure. Just be patient.

You need not visit India or Egypt to win esoteric enlightenment. You can find it right in your own mind. And it is really marvelous the way it happens. You can go just as far as you really want to go.

## The True Purpose of Life

Enlightened men are often accused of being impractical dreamers. I hear this so many times at my lectures that I can often tell the exact words to be used.

Research proves otherwise. Henry David Thoreau, considered an idler by some, could be a highly practical merchant in his pencil and graphite firm. Plato was a successful salesman to his Egyptian customers. Jacob Boehme, in addition to being hailed as a mystical genius, was known in his native Gorlitz as a master businessman and shoemaker. John Burroughs, the American nature-philosopher, was an efficient bank examiner.

It is all a matter of *values*. What do you consider valuable? That question is answered by every man by the way he spends his mental money — his inner thoughts.

Let's examine false values.

Suppose a man was somehow under the delusion that his very life depended upon his eating potatoes every day. Regardless of an abundance of other foods, he clings to his unrealistic passion for potatoes.

Now, you can be sure that this man will be whirled about by worries. He will be critical, harsh and competitive with anyone whom he suspects is out to limit his potatoes. He will most likely join SOPP — the Society of Potato Protectors.

Amusing? Men have identified themselves with far more foolish causes!

Foolish? Of course. But never forget, he falsely assumes he is fighting for his very life!

How can he awaken to his folly, and so erase the pain? First, he must become disgusted with pain. Then, he can experiment. He can gradually do without potatoes until *he sees the truth for himself*. With that, potato-passion falls away of itself. That is the basic system by which all artificial values are destroyed.

19

The following queries from one of my students and my responses illustrate for you the cosmic goals to pursue.

**Q:** How can I create the desire to be free?

**A:** You do not need to create it; you already have it. As a matter of fact, you cannot escape it no matter what you do. Your part is to awaken to it, become increasingly aware of its call, and to answer that call with a mounting *yes*.

**Q:** But why is it so hard to do?

**A:** It is hard because we don't know it is easy, like a man paddling his boat because he doesn't *see* the motor. If he will abandon his frantic paddling, he can turn around and see the motor. You have nothing to *do*, only something to see. This is a basic teaching of Zen.

**Q:** But there is so much to learn!

**A:** Don't worry about the landslide of principles given you to work upon. Absorb them as best you can for now, easily and without concern. They are like marbles crowded into the mouth of a funnel. Eventually, they will drop through the opening, one by one, to be clearly seen and understood.

**Q:** Nothing confuses me more than my goal in life. I would breathe easier if I could just clarify my purpose.

**A:** All right, breathe easily. In your Outer World, have any goal you like. Be an industrial executive, an artist, world traveler; it makes no difference. In your Inner World, never think you have any goal other than to return to your natural self. That is the only goal which makes any difference.

## What Man is Really Like

At the very start, we must see the actual condition of men and women, and not see them as they *appear* to be or as ideals say they *should* be. Man suffers from a split self. He seeks security in people and possessions, at the same time sensing their emptiness. He has an urge to find himself but is afraid of what self-examination will reveal. The more changes he makes, the more he remains the same. He thumpingly declares that he will do something, then promptly does the opposite. He feels himself a gigantic fake. He wants desperately to share himself with others but has nothing of his real self to share. His smile has a worried look. He tries to lose his anxiety in distracting activities and fears the silence when they end. No matter what he does, it is always the wrong thing.

Most of all, he is afraid, terribly afraid. His nervousness pressures him into seeking excitements which he hopes will hold at bay the agonizing inner crisis. But he never wins. Sooner or later, he is overpowered and cast down once more.

Picture a patient on his way to the doctor's office. He dallies, distracted here and there by interesting sights, a newspaper headline. Then, as the novelty wears off, he becomes conscious of his illness and continues on to the doctor's. For the next hour or two he swings back and forth between distraction and pain, until he finally realizes he had better get on his way to the cure.

The human quest for wholeness is like that. We are distracted by thrills, impulsive desires, false doctrines, and most of all, by our pretense that everything is just fine, when we secretly know everything is all wrong. But at one point or another, the pain becomes unendurable and our pretenses are shattered. With a sigh of relief, we stop playing and head for the sure cure at the office of reality.

How does the great change start?

The first spark of awareness that there is *something entirely different* marks the turning point of your life. Before, you did not notice anything beyond your usual life. For instance, you assumed that all you could do with mental pain was to either express or suppress it. But that single, tiny spark, coming at an unexpected moment, has awakened you to strangely new possibilities.

That is all it lasted, just a split second. Then you fell

asleep again, perhaps for a week or month or year, before it sparked again. But never mind how long it takes for the next glimpse. You have seen something. You have become conscious for a split second.

Now, nothing will ever be the same again. Seized by reality, you are on the way. The path back, you will find, is a combination of new shocks, deeper dismays, fresh wonderments and happy revelations. And all the while you come closer and closer to your own inner quietness, just as the depths of the sea are calm, in spite of raging storms overhead.

As Ralph Waldo Emerson writes:

*The soul's communication of truth is the highest event in nature ... and this communication is an influx of the Divine Mind into our mind .... Every moment when the individual feels invaded by it is memorable.*

It is a mistake for anyone to think he has lived too long in his old, unsatisfactory ways to make the great change. If you switch on the light in a dark room, it makes no difference how long it was dark because the light will still shine. *Be teachable.* That is the whole secret.

## How Esoteric Truths Elevate You

"Know thyself" is an essential first step. The trouble is, we wrongly take knowledge of our superficial habits as self-understanding. We fail to see that our surface habits not only misrepresent the true self, but also are often compulsive and damaging. Clear understanding of a harmful habit erases it.

We must understand falseness because it consists of everything about us that is strained, unnatural and unnecessary. It is all the imitative habits that make us mechanical, instead of spontaneous. For instance, a man might appear to be the self-confident life-of-the-party, when he is actually lonely and haunted. A woman might drive herself into social activities, not because she really enjoys them, but because she is afraid to stop running.

To our rescue comes our real self, our essential nature, or the Supermind. It consists of everything natural and relaxed.

One type of falseness exhibited by people concerns willpower. What is commonly called willpower is nothing more than the temporary domination of one desire over another. A man desires to eat less in order to lose weight, but an hour later he is overwhelmed by a contrary desire for candy. But there is such a thing as real willpower. It comes as we live from the basic self, not from conflicting desires.

We think and behave wrongly because we have not acquired knowledge of the Supermind. For instance, stop thinking that you must sacrifice yourself to anyone in order to get friendship, marriage, success, money, excitement, sex, achievement, relief, romance, comfort, strength, security, energy, relaxation, popularity, power, pleasure or anything else. You must not pay 99 cents in order to get a penny.

Do just this much. Stop sacrificing yourself in order to get these things. When you have done so, you will understand why it was essential to your happiness.

Do not confuse lack of knowledge with lack of intelligence. They are different items. Intelligence is the gathering and grasping of knowledge. A man is not stupid because he fails to understand the workings of a space rocket; he merely lacks information. If interested in space rockets, he could use his intelligence to collect knowledge. I mention this because many people feel themselves incapable of grasping cosmic facts. This is not so, because by seeing that intelligence is the patient gathering of knowledge, anyone can confidently gain self-transforming information.

However, *esoteric facts by themselves cannot awaken a man*. A *mentally memorized* fact is not the same as the *psychic realization* of that fact! This accounts for people who are familiar with religious teachings, but whose private lives are shaky. Such people need more than a storehouse of bare facts. They need the kind of psychic sight which leads to inner alteration. We can know a thousand facts about religion and not know a single fact about ourselves.

The greatest tragedy is that everyone assumes he already knows himself. This must be worked against constantly. The most tragic deception is self-deception.

Esoteric truths resemble a coded message which must be deciphered by people eager enough to get the message.

## The Way to True Cosmic Guidance

A confused person exclaims, "But I don't know what to *believe!*"

To which the enlightened teacher replies, "Why believe? Just *see!*"

Certainly it is possible to see. And then you *know*. The famous lines of William Blake explains, *If the doors of perception were cleansed, everything would appear to man as it is — infinite.*

Certainly there are men whose psychic sight enables them to see things as they are. We meet many of them in this book. Plotinus, a famed Greek mystic whose inner light projected itself outwardly for all to see, is an excellent historical example.

He was born in Egypt in A.D. 204 and after traveling in the East, absorbing its esoteric wisdom, he settled in Rome. Founding a philosophical school, Plotinus soon attracted fame as a teacher and writer. Hearing of his psychic intelligence and gracious character, the famous people of the day sought him out. His visitors included the royal couple, Emperor Gallienus and Empress Salonina. His home was a haven of rest amidst the alarms and chaos of warring Rome.

*Enneads*, the writing of Plotinus, deeply inspired Augustine, Dante, and other thinkers who followed him.

And no wonder, when Plotinus wrote:

*When we meet with the self thus purified, and see the entire self as a single radiance, a radiance beyond measure ... the vision has come. Even while here below, we have attained the heights, and need no further guidance.*

Guidance? Here is the entire secret: Quietly pass through each hour as if you don't care what happens to your happiness. Do this not with what is commonly called carelessness, but because you wisely see that you need not care.

*Understand and do this as far as your Inner World is concerned, and you will have no behavior problems in the Outer World.* The reason we have exterior problems is because we seek guidance from the ego (self), which is nothing but a mass of confusions.

Friedrich Nietzsche declared, *To learn to look away from oneself is necessary in order to see many things. Can you get out of your own way?* That is the only question, the only problem, the only solution.

There is something in you that can stand perfectly still and calmly watch everything that happens around you. It is like a revolving beam from a lighthouse that casts light on surrounding storms, but is perfectly unaffected and stands undaunted.

When you see things as they really are, the Outer World cannot affect your peace in any way whatsoever. If it occurs to one man in a million that he can be poor, alone, unsuccessful, in poor health, and still be happy, that one man is a true genius.

## How to Know That All is Well

**Q:** I work along the lines you suggest, but still run into one confusion after another. Why?

**A:** You do not as yet see your own wrong thinking as the cause. To experience the painful consequences of false ideas is not the same as seeing yourself as the originator.

See yourself as the cause of your conditions. That is the beginning of the end of trouble.

**Q:** In your lectures you urge us to enjoy ourselves, yet all around we see so much sadness and badness. How can life be fun?

**A:** *Life* is fun, but your conditioned *thoughts about it* are not. Do not assume that your ideas toward life constitute life itself. When you truly see life as it is, it is enjoyment — a new kind.

Learning to listen to the inner call can be illustrated like this: A seaman, lost in an island jungle, hopes to hear the roar of the waves as a guide back to the sea. He listens as best he can, but jungle noises of animals and winds block his hearing. But he persists in alertness as he wanders about. Suddenly, as the jungle falls silent for a moment, he hears the faint but definite sound of the sea.

At this point he knows that all is well. Even when the jungle noises distract him temporarily, he still knows that he is headed in the right direction.

Likewise, when the unnatural mind ceases its frantic struggle and falls silent, we hear the guiding voice that was trying to reach us all the time.

Count Leo Tolstoy, who saw the light, points out:

*Men need but understand this: they need but stop troubling themselves about external and general matters, in which they are not free, and use but one hundredth part of the energy ... on the recognition and profession of the truth which stands before them, on the emancipation of themselves ....*

When anxious thinking, planning and deciding come to an end, anxiety also terminates. The conditioned mind has no answer to anything. Sooner or later we must come to this realization. We must see by observation and experience that this is an actual fact.

When you are at the end of your mental rope, when you

do not know what to do or think, when every attempted escape is blocked, when all is despair, why struggle with the problem when your mind is incapable of finding a solution? Why do you continue to think at all? Somehow we sense that all would be well if we could only get our frantic mind out of the way. The deeper part of us feels that the mind struggling to free itself from a problem is the very problem itself.

Why not step quietly aside and watch what happens when the conditioned mind ceases to struggle? Do that much and watch what happens.

*The Supermind begins where the ordinary mind ends.*

# Important Points from Chapter 1

1. Anyone can awaken to his natural Supermind freedom and peace.

2. The Supermind operates far above ordinary human conditioned thoughts.

3. Supermind-thinking is the only practical way to live.

4. Your Inner World determines your Outer World.

5. For true happiness, place your Inner World first.

6. The great purpose of life is to wake up to Cosmic Truth.

7. You can return to your natural calm and relaxation.

8. Never sacrifice your inner integrity to anyone.

9. We must go beyond mere conditioned knowledge to psychic insight.

10. Allow true cosmic guidance to arise from within yourself.

# 2

## How to Use Your Supermind for New Successes

Some years ago an Egyptian woman was strolling on the banks of the Nile. Her curiosity was aroused by some broken pieces of clay, which had strange markings. Sensing a valuable discovery, she brought the pieces to authorities for examination. They proved of great value indeed, being ancient letters of Pharaoh Akhenaton.

Supposing that woman, upon sighting the pieces, had merely reacted, "How curious," and passed on her way. She would never have known what she missed!

Millions of people do exactly this. And, that is why there are millions of panicky people.

You must avoid this. Do not take a merely curious or even philosophical view of the ideas encountered in this chapter. *Wholeheartedly receive them.* Treasure them and be utterly *practical*. Make them of as much use as you would your dinner.

A real philosopher is not one who goes around quoting airy ideas. As Henry David Thoreau stated:

*To be a philosopher is not merely to have subtle thoughts, nor even to found a school, but so to love wisdom as to live, according to its dictates, a life of simplicity, independence, magnanimity and trust.*

Thoreau's key word is *live* — but live fully!

How can you start?

Break away. Do it by short steps, if necessary, but break away. No, you won't succeed the first week. There are too many people around you who will screech when you dare to leave them alone in their prison. They don't want you to get out; they want you to be as miserable as they. Your daring is an exposure of their weakness.

Don't look for someone in whom to believe. Believe in yourself. The only authentic authority is your own original nature. And, I will add, it is the only genuinely compassionate authority.

Think of your search as the recovery of a precious gem which you have temporarily misplaced.

Your secret psychic and cosmic self is supreme against all human odds!

## The Chief Illusion of Man

A fable from the ancient East tells of a wealthy but evil magician who owned large flocks of sheep. Not wanting to build expensive fences or hire shepherds, he devised a clever scheme. He hypnotized the sheep and told them all sorts of lies about their identities. He convinced one sheep that he was a lion, another that he was an eagle, and so on. He also hypnotized them into believing that everything he did to them was for their own good and that no harm could come their way as long as they trusted him. So the gullible sheep served the selfish purposes of the wicked magician.

Thus are men hypnotized also. The evil magician is their own set of false illusions. They not only think illusions are good for them, but haven't the slightest notion of their hypnotic state! *While they dream, they do not know that they are dreaming.* (Chuang-tse)

29

The chief illusion of man, that which breeds all others, is a false sense of self. A man is not who he thinks he is. Scottish philosopher David Hume points out, *The identity, which we ascribe to the mind of man, is a factitious one ....* This is so vital to grasp that we meet it frequently in this book. But for now, we can say this: Don't be afraid to let go of this acquired, invented identity, this false feeling of "I." That is like being afraid to let go of a headache. That is what the imaginary "I" is — one great big headache.

When you first begin to suspect that you are not the person you think you are, you become increasingly disturbed. Disregard this as it is merely a cunning trick of the false self wanting to hang onto its fake existence at your expense. By patiently enduring the disturbance, you proceed to another great region — *understanding* — which is victory.

*Hence it follows incontrovertibly, that one who uses his understanding aright can fall a prey to no sorrow.*
(Baruch Spinoza)

Because there is no such thing as the usually conceived human self, there is also no such thing as human strength or weakness, wisdom or stupidity, success or defeat, goodness or evil, or other opposites like these. *Nothing belongs to us; all belongs to God, to Supermind, or to whatever name you choose to call ultimate reality.*

## The Right Kind of Rebellion

Imaginary identities create chaos within a person's psychological system. They cause conflict, like two rams battering each other. A person may have an unconscious picture of himself being so "strong" that he is not bothered by sex passions. When sex thoughts pass through his mind, as they will, he wrongly calls them "evil." Having labeled them as his own evil thoughts, he feels guilty and ashamed. He then tries to repress or deny them, and the more he does, the greater his agony. He does not see that he must let thoughts pass through his mind without identification,

30

judgment, condemnation or any other reaction. Now he is behaving in the intelligent way which cannot create conflict. There is conflict only when an artificial identity clashes with what actually occurs.

As the invented or man-made self disappears, painful thinking also vanishes. One such phantom is thinking that someone or something is chaining you down, restricting your opportunities for advancement or enjoyment. Such faulty thinking is always accompanied by painful resentment toward those felt to be responsible for the chains. And that leads to useless rebellion, much like smashing a violin because our own playing of it produces disharmony.

No one person can "restrict" any other person. Not when you really understand. The chains exist only in faulty thinking.

But there is a place in your quest for rebellion — the right kind of rebellion. Rebel against everything within yourself that you feel is artificial. Become what you are!

You see, there is a vast difference between what the false self *thinks* and what the true self *knows*. So welcome self-exposure as you would welcome a purifying breeze in a stuffy room. Learn what you are really like, for then you learn what you can really be with the cosmic or Supermind. It is not as disastrous as we might suppose to see our own nothingness; it is actually fulfillment. It only *seems like disaster* because of our fearful hesitancy to give up the false ego-self. We pass through this dark tunnel by first entering it.

No idea you could grasp will do more to free you from unnecessary burdens, including false guilts and duties. Human egotism is hell on earth. How much of the synthetic human self have you allowed to fall away from you today? That is the test of today's success.

## Why We Must Go Beyond Human Thought

Life clears itself to the degree that we understand how the mind works. Human thinking is the process of comparing things. On the everyday level, comparison is useful. In buying a home you compare several, selecting the one best for you.

But there is no place for comparison in your inner life. If you call one thing good, you must also call its opposite bad. Then, if the bad comes your way, you suffer. If you call it good when you receive a cheery letter, you will feel bad when no letter comes. If you feel elated over your youthfulness, you will feel depressed at the thought of growing older. *Where there is good, there must be evil.* (Lu Wang)

Our thinking must not be influenced by these painful opposites, but rather it must generate from the awareness of the Supermind. We must go beyond both the good and bad conceived by human thinking. Beyond it we find a new Good.

To think from the opposites of good and bad is to be spiritually asleep. In this state of sleep a man tears himself apart by trying to be what he thinks is good and avoiding what he thinks is bad. But it is impossible to be humanly good or bad, for of our human selves, we have neither. *There is only Cosmic Goodness!* Every true religion teaches this, but few see it.

What a revelation! This means you should never feel bad about your own supposed badness. That is the very thing that perpetuates it. Fear of badness means that you *identify* yourself with it; that is, you assume you are your own badness, which you are not. Of your human self, you are neither good nor bad. But all this must be searched out until you see its esoteric meaning. Listen to the following dialogue:

**Q:** Please show how this applies in the practical situation of friendships and social relations.

**A:** When you are free from thinking in opposites, you neither accept nor reject anyone in the usual meaning of those terms. You are free of the loneliness involved in rejection and the conflicts that often come in accepting involvement with people. This provides a totally new kind of acceptance toward everyone, which is genuine love.

**Q:** I'm sensitive to what others think of me!

**A:** How on earth can another's thought about you harm you? It is *your* thought about *his* thought that harms. Change *your* thought.

A chief cause of unhappiness is what I call *mental movies*. Mental movies are a misuse of the imagination. You know how it goes. You have a painful experience with someone, then run it over and over in your mind. You visualize what you said, what he did, how you both felt. As awful as it is, you feel compelled to repeat the film day and night. It is as if you were locked inside a theater playing a horror movie.

To break out, be aware that you *are* running a mental movie. Be conscious of its mechanical hold on your mind. Then, by deliberate choice, break it off. Shake your head and break it off. Now, at this instant, take a quick look. Where is your pain? It is not there. It has disappeared. You have now accomplished something great. You have proved that you *can* snap the film and its tyrannical pain. You are free and you are free *right now*.

Try the above method for yourself. Even though you succeed at first for just a split second, you have succeeded completely! Now realizing that small success is possible, you can advance to great success!

## Secrets for a Successful Search of Self

We must learn to ask correct questions, like "Why do I behave as I do?" and "How can I stop wasting my natural forces?" These are right questions, for their aim is self-development. As an example of a wrong question, someone asks, "I'm nervous over a forthcoming event. How should I act when there?"

We can never know how to act correctly as long as we still live with a mind filled with false ideas and contradictory desires. Such a mind is always nervous and uncertain. But when living from the Supermind, we know exactly how to act in every situation. As Sri Ramakrishna remarked, *Gold is gold, no matter where you place it.* Incidentally, Supermind-thinking keeps us out of anxious situations in the first place.

Learn to work for your own true benefit. The victorious life can be compared to a walled garden. Beauty and fragrance are there, but must be earned. There is no wide gate open to the public, for the garden would soon be trampled upon by the merely curious and by those who fail to truly value its splendor. The wall must be scaled with personal effort, for that is the test of sincerity. Does the seeker want the garden enough to exert himself in an attempt to gain it? If so, he will return again and again, despite failure after failure, regardless of the seeming hopelessness of his task, and he will abandon all useless possessions that make him too heavy to climb the wall successfully.

A major problem of the seeker is his inability to distinguish true sources of aid from false ones. In his bewilderment, he stumbles from one system or teacher to another, often falling victim to useless or dangerous doctrines. His hopes are raised to the heights of elation, but before long he tumbles down once more, to begin another wearisome search.

He can help himself. For one thing, he can see his present inability to judge between the real and the unreal. He can observe how his anxiety drives him into acceptance of

34

anything promising quick relief. He can see that he is mistakenly placing emotional thrills before mental clarity. *By seeing his own helplessness, he has revealed to himself a fact of gigantic benefit.* By first detecting weakness in himself, he can then go on to discover true strength!

Do not be impatient with your seemingly slow progress. Do not try to run faster than you presently can. If you are studying, reflecting *and trying,* you are making progress whether you are aware of it or not. A traveler walking the road in the darkness of night is still going forward. Someday, some way, everything will break open, like the natural unfolding of a rosebud.

As we gradually come closer to home, we recognize it. There is a feeling of something vaguely familiar about everything, like visiting our home town after a long absence. We sense a new closeness to where we used to be. John Greenleaf Whittier expresses it very well in his poem, *A Mystery:*

*No clue of memory led me on*
*But well the ways I knew;*
*A feeling of familiar things*
*With every footstep grew.*

## How to Win the Truly Valuable Gain Through Loss

We now take up a psychic law which the human mind resists with all its might. Yet, when received and understood, it provides the inspired life.

It is the law of *gain through voluntary loss.* In order to gain the new and superior, we must first lose the old and inferior. In the physical world, an old chair and a new chair cannot occupy the same space at the same time. Likewise in the psychic world. The mind has no room for both a true and false idea; one or the other must be there.

35

For us to win the truly valuable, we must willingly give up the shallow and invaluable. A story will illustrate the point. It is retold from the *Gulistan*, or *Rose Garden*, the Persian classic, by Saadi.

Two friends, both the sons of Amirs, were in Egypt to pursue their goals. One of them devoted his efforts to the attainment of wealth and political power. He succeeded, eventually becoming an Egyptian prince. The other son sought the fruits of science and mysticism, also succeeding. When the prince scorned his friend's lowly position, the philosopher replied, "I am grateful for having ignored worldly fortune in favor of true wisdom. For one thing, I do not possess the power to harm mankind."

Will you voluntarily let go of the old, the shallow, the useless, without demanding to know the nature of the new? That is the challenge at every step toward the Supermind. Let the following questions and answers show you how to proceed:

**Q:** You say that esoteric ideas are simple to grasp, yet they seem difficult. Why?

**A:** An idea can be simple and yet not clear. Simplicity is in the idea itself, misunderstanding is in the mind. When the mind becomes clear, so does the idea.

**Q:** I still don't know how to become a "self-aware" person. Is there a practical technique I can practice?

**A:** Jot down every strong impression you see in yourself during your day. Collect only the stronger, more emotional ones. Note them briefly, like *annoyed by weather* and *elated by good news*. Before bedtime, review the passing parade you observed. This makes you aware of the contents of consciousness, which changes you.

**Q:** I want to help others.

**A:** Please don't go around trying to save the world. You have all you can do to save yourself.

# Twenty Basic and Supreme Principles of Supermind

1. To recognize and dissolve the false sense of self is a brave and rewarding task.

2. *The help you need is always available, but you must want it, receive it, work sincerely and persistently.*

3. Your central self is totally untouched by grief, confusion, desperation.

4. *It is possible for any man or woman to achieve constructive self-change in a fantastic way, a way presently unseen.*

5. You transform your life by understanding your desires, rather than by attempting to gratify them.

6. *Real courage is to tell yourself what you don't want to hear.*

7. Do not accept the inferior in the belief that it is the best you can do.

8. *Just as a fruitful branch extends from the tree trunk, so does personal stability come out of esoteric knowledge.*

9. Invented values bring despair; natural values bring freedom.

10. *If you don't like the effect, don't produce the cause.*

11. Punishment comes only from false thoughts; therefore, to stop punishment, stop illusory thoughts.

12. *The way you react to daily events is exactly what makes your day what it is.*

13. The truth is a very serious threat to misery.

14. *A nagging dissatisfaction with slavery proves the existence of liberty.*

15. Within you at this very moment is everything you seek, but you must awaken to it.

16. *Do not let yourself be attracted by anything but Cosmic, Supermind Truth.*

17. Never struggle to change your conditions. Instead, seek a change in your level of consciousness, or awareness of Cosmic Truth.

18. *Anything you get from another human being that requires a sacrifice of your integrity is not worth getting.*

19. You can do a thousand times better than you think you can.

20. *The grand purpose of life is to wake up to the Cosmic Truths of Supermind.*

Let your familiarity with the teachings of *Supermind* turn into acceptance and understanding. Do not unconsciously or subconsciously oppose the unfamiliar as it may appear to you. A Western reader might find Eastern mystic ideas, like those of Zen and Vedanta, somewhat strange at first. But eventually, he will see that many Western teachings include Eastern mystic thought, including those of Swiss psychiatrist Carl Jung, and those of Ralph Waldo Emerson, the great humanist.

An architect was commissioned by his friend and employer to build a new home. Wanting only the best for his life-long friend, the architect poured his best effort into the project. Whenever there was a choice between good and mediocre materials, the finest was used. If best results could be obtained only by spending an extra day in a particular task, he spent that extra day.

When the fine home was finished, the employer held a celebration. After dinner, he presented the home to the architect in honor of his many years of faithful service, who had unknowingly, but actually, built it for himself!

Select only the best for yourself. You already sense what it is by following the guidance in this book.

## How to Get The Power of Understanding

Suppose a child in Los Angeles writes his first letter, intended for a young friend in London. Knowing nothing about the postal system, the child wonders how his letter can reach its destination across thousands of miles of land and sea. Lacking knowledge, he worries and asks anxious questions. But when the process is explained, he sees how everything works for him, and so relaxes. Because he *understands*, he need no longer *think*. (Remember this great truth.)

Do you see why this book stresses esoteric understanding? It cancels the need for worried thinking.

The vast majority of men and women in the world do not understand, but *assume* that they do. It is illustrated by a humorous but devastating remark by a relatively unknown German thinker, Max Stirner. Stirner commented that men arrogantly wander about the grounds of their madhouse, not realizing where they are, because the grounds of it are so large!

When encountering an esoteric truth you do not understand, the correct reaction is, "Now, then, exactly what is this trying to tell me?"

Esoteric knowledge clears up every confusion created by lack of understanding. Take worldly prosperity. Cosmic progress does not require you to abandon the people or possessions in your life. You need only give up your identification with them, that is, you must drop the fleeting excitements they create. When this is achieved, you have a spiritual indifference toward them, for you realize that mere excitements add nothing to your eternal self. You also see that exciting feelings always react with their opposite — to feelings of pain. When free of both excitement and pain regarding people and possessions, you enjoy them without fearing their loss.

Understanding frees us from that terrible tyrant, frustration. As long as a man tries to do the impossible, frustration must continue. The impossible consists of trying to force life to conform to false psychological needs, such as praise and approval from others. In the Outer World you have the true needs of food, rest, physical comfort. In the Inner World you have but one true need — unity with your Supermind. This is best illustrated in the following:

**Q:** How can I know when I have understood a certain truth?

**A:** When you no longer repeat the same mistakes, like feeling envious and demanding attention. Your mistakes are based on misunderstanding. When you really perceive a higher fact, you no longer need to behave in the old ways. You abandon the muddy road when you sight the highway.

**Q:** You say we are free and always have been free. I don't understand. I am not free of doubt and distress.

**A:** There is a world of difference — literally a *world* of difference — between a cosmic fact and your awareness of it. It is a fact that tomatoes are good food, but people once rejected them, and so could not experience their goodness. Awareness is everything. It makes a fact personally operative.

**Q:** Thanks to your books I have made considerable progress, but it is a long, long road. What should I do when I get tired?

**A:** Be indifferent to your tiredness and remember that the truth is the only thing that never gets tired of putting up with you.

## Let Yourself Flow Forward

For those who have learned wrongly, the path is clear: *Unlearn the negative.*

Take the seeming injustices of life as an example. Many people feel that their efforts to live honorably are unrewarded and unappreciated, while unpleasant people prosper. Some feel they have been kindly to others, only to be mistreated in return.

There is injustice on the human level, but our aim is to live above it. On the higher level, you will be astonished to find that feelings of injustice or mistreatment simply do not exist. Such words lose their meaning; you lose all sense of grievance.

It all depends upon what we love. If our ruling passion is for higher life, what do we care whether people reward or appreciate us or not? It makes no difference. A soaring eagle has no need to be appreciated by ground creatures.

A certain sign of deepened understanding is when you no longer criticize unkind or troublesome people, but feel sorry for them. You realize that no one can get away with badness, that unkind people are their own punishment. Since you have escaped self-punishment through your own new insights, you now see that others must do likewise. And so you are kindly to the unkind.

Incidentally, you should be very grateful to people who hurt you by doing you wrong. They provide the stimulus needed for probing just why you feel wronged, which frees you of the pain of feeling wronged.

Develop the habit of turning inward whenever something goes wrong outwardly. We are so anxious to protest or make a telephone call or change something. Reverse it. Think, "Now, there is something within me quite capable of handling this without useless motions." Constant practice reveals that there is.

When a man catches his first glimpse of what it means to live above his usual mechanical and negative reactions to life, he feels a *new pleasure*. And he senses an entirely new kind of opportunity.

Have you ever felt a lack of opportunity for crashing through the maze of your mind? Give yourself the opportunity by asking, "What would it be like if I ceased struggling to live my life and just let it be lived for me? What if I simply dropped the whole painful business of trying to be happy or popular or wise? What would happen?"

*Do not try to imagine what would happen.* And do not react timidly toward the idea. Instead, experiment.

Experiment right now, right where you are holding this book. Decide that from this moment on you will make no further efforts to find happiness. You will not seek excitement or call on friends or do anything else you usually do to make yourself feel good.

Instead, let yourself be led to do whatever happens by itself. Do not try to think; let your thoughts think for you. Let go. Drop all initiative. Let yourself flow.

At first, this causes uneasiness. Never mind. It is only because you have never tried it before. Stick with it throughout the hours and days. Don't try to live; let yourself be lived.

I know what miracle will occur if you persist in this. I cannot communicate it to you, but I urge you to experiment for yourself. Then, you will know the miracle for yourself.

## How to Brighten Your Real Self

We must not miss the point of life, which is self-realization. Growth comes if we make the right choices. If we choose self-knowledge instead of self-deception, we float upward. If we select quiet examination of suffering, instead of resistance, we move away from suffering. If we prefer reliance upon internal authority, rather than upon external voices, we brighten the self.

The conditioned mind suspects that all these things are too good to be true. It feels it would be nice if such wonders could be achieved here and now, but fears they are nothing more than pretty ideals.

The conditioned mind is wrong. I assure you that all these wonders are true and possible.

You may ask, "But how do I learn to think from the lofty level of the Supermind?"

Every sincere effort toward cosmic consciousness works for self-realization, but try this specific technique: *Observe what you think is necessary for you to say and do.* Practiced faithfully, it is as revealing as reading your own biography written by a friend who knows you intimately.

Let's take an example of self-awareness in action. In previous pages we saw that you need not have the slightest concern with what happens to you. Now, this is a fact, but will give you mixed reactions. Part of you will feel thrilled at its truth, but another part will confusedly wonder how it could be true of you personally.

By being aware of your resistance, awareness does its good work. You are then left with the truth and nothing but the truth. So awareness of every reaction is your final freedom.

Rapid progress is assured when you try to discover your real motive for doing something, as opposed to the "supposed" motive. At first you will discover them far apart, but with self-unity, they become one and the same.

Honesty is the only policy. It reveals, as Krishnamurti points out, the true as true and the false as false. If we seek out spiritual ideals merely for a comforting confirmation of what we wish to believe, we are not seeking but wandering.

The motto of the sincere seeker is clear enough: "The truth at all cost." What are the costs? We must let the truth cost us everything belonging to the theatrical stage, especially the tiresome act of pretending that we already know the truth.

It is more honest to weep than to laugh. But if you will weep consciously, you will finally laugh honestly.

There is true magic and there is false magic. False magic is when a man wants something, employs some superstitious mental gimmick to get it, then proudly believes he brought it about through his gimmick. People excitedly tell you of the appearance of something for which they prayed, but don't tell you of dozens of non-appearances.

What is true magic? Living in harmony with Supermind.

A man's internal state resembles a battlefield where two armies engage in constant combat. One army seeks spiritual victory, while the other opposes it fiercely. Man suffers from this psychic civil war, just as external warfare produces victims. Back and forth the battle rages, with man shouting jubilantly when winning a skirmish, only to fall back in mournful defeat an hour later.

Is this his necessary fate? Is this all there is? No. There is something else. There is a third force capable of turning the tide of battle in his favor.

We meet this powerful ally in the following chapter and learn what it can do for us.

## Summary of Vital Ideas

1. Your own original Cosmic nature is your true authority.

2. No one on earth can bar you from genuine values of Cosmic Truth.

3. Let your false sense of self fade away with Supermind.

4. Refuse to be a victim of painful mental movies.

5. True strength follows the admission of weakness.

6. Your central self is untouched by pain and grief.

7. Esoteric understanding cancels worried thinking.

8. The Cosmic Truth never gets tired of putting up with you.

9. Supermind-living provides new kinds of satisfying pleasures.

10. You need have no anxious concern for yourself in any way when you trust your Supermind.

# 3

## How to Get at the Turning Point of Your Life for All Success

If you truly wish, the revelations in this chapter can mark the great turning point of your life.

Of all the questions asked by seekers, one stands out above all others. People say, "I want to succeed with the higher life, but *how?*"

Let me answer with a single word — *receptivity* — then explore with you its magnificent and wealthy meaning.

### Receptivity

Individual receptivity is absolutely everything. Without it, nothing changes. With it, all things are possible for you.

Contact with the truth brings out either the best or the worst in a man. When we hear a truth, it falls either on the true self or the false self. If it falls on the artificial self, it will be rejected, distorted or ignored, doing no good for the individual. But if a person has a welcoming attitude, the truth falls on his authentic self, providing understanding and relief.

Receptivity is a matter of degree. Our task is to set out the welcome mat more and more, enabling it to increasingly aid us. A little receptivity opens the way for more, for each rewarding experience shows us that the truth we once feared and rejected is the very happiness we want.

Are you capable of receiving what you really want? If you can answer that question in the affirmative, you can have everything you really want.

Receptivity is a miracle worker. It changes the way you see everything. Take what is commonly called failure. It is necessary for you to voluntarily fail, fail, fail so many times without resistance that you finally see that failure is only a word, an attitude, a feeling and nothing more.

In the realm of social contacts, you should be so receptive that every contact with another person reveals something new about yourself. The best teachers are those who are the worst off; the unkind people who are negative, complaining, talkative, boring, boastful.

## How to Be Calm in a Crisis

Here is a new view that is the rich result of receptivity. A man gains insight into his false ideas and these melt under such discernment. Nothing else will change him. Exterior moralities, preachings, authorities, all are in vain. Just as Columbus dared to disprove the theory of a flat earth, a man must dare to prove himself wrong. Then, he is right.

A clever salesman might persuade a customer that a certain pair of boots are just right for rugged mountain-climbing, but in a practical test the customer finds them powerless to protect him from pain from rugged rocks. He sees for himself the difference between what he believed was true and what is the actual fact.

That is what suffering attempts to show us. We suffer because we refuse to see the difference between truth and falsehood, between human fancy and spiritual fact. We close our eyes to the inadequacy of our present boots which do not hide the pain! Suffering tries to teach the lesson, "Look, you are not living according to reality because you prefer your illusions. To be happy, rid yourself of the inadequate boots. Admit they hurt; toss them out. Now you are ready for the right ones and you won't hurt any more."

The German mystical genius, Meister Eckhart, compares the readiness of seekers to loaves of bread in the following:

*Suppose four loaves are placed in an oven, one each of oats, barley, rye and wheat. Although the same heat is given to all four, some loaves turn out superior to others. The heat is not to blame for the inferior loaves; the fault lies in the very nature of the loaves which resisted the beneficial heat.*

Use this special secret for developing receptivity: Learn to love situations which make you uncomfortable. That is the only way you can learn to be comfortable everywhere. Never seek to protect your inner self in a crisis. Let it shake you up any way it likes, while you calmly stand aside and watch. When you totally permit this to occur, you can never be shaken again by life.

Willingly listen to a true teacher. We cannot gain what a teacher has to give unless we submit our mistaken ideas to him for destruction. If we withhold, conceal, argue or defend, we make it impossible for him to give us what we need.

## Esoteric Gems Are for the Asking

We are wise when we listen to true teachers for, as the Persian poet Saadi points out, *You should know that foolish people are a hundred times more unwilling to meet the wise, than the wise are reluctant for the company of the foolish.*

Imagine yourself and a temperamental friend driving along the highway toward a particular destination, perhaps a restaurant. You know the way, but your friend who is behind the wheel does not. When you offer him guidance, he irritably refuses to listen, insisting that he already knows. Even after a dozen wrong turns, he still rejects your guidance.

What would you do? You would wisely remain silent, realizing that only he can solve his problem. You hope his repeated mistakes will compel him to acknowledge that he really does not know, after which he will listen to you. As for your own state of mind, it is entirely at ease. After all, *you* are not lost.

So it is in the spiritual life. Truth cannot and will not force itself upon anyone because the unnatural part of man always attacks and distorts an unwanted truth. We can only have what we actually want, not what we *say* or *think* we want. This is why a true teacher never gives esoteric gems unless the seeker first asks. Here are some deep questions people have asked and my answers to them:

**Q:** Many people study religion and philosophy, but that doesn't seem to make them any happier. Why don't their studies pay off?

**A:** That is the whole tragedy. I encounter it every day. People desperately ask questions about life without the slightest awareness of their *incapacity to receive* the answers. And, when they hear a true answer, but fail to grasp it, they sadly assume that no answer exists. Non-receptivity is their tragedy.

**Q:** You have made me aware of my foolish following of the ideas of others. How can I break this dependency?

**A:** To do this you must challenge every idea presented to you. If all the world believes that two and two make five, you know it still makes four and must courageously insist upon it.

**Q:** Is there really an answer to the mystery of life?
**A:** Of course there is.

## The True Guidance of Supermind

Waves of power from the Supermind try to reach us constantly. They seek entrance in order to guide, heal and comfort, but our inner noisiness blocks their beneficial influence, just as a person chattering endlessly on his telephone cuts himself off from incoming calls. We block our incoming cosmic good through Supermind by our refusal to give up our false identification, and by our fickle desires.

Let me explain the esoteric meaning of the New Testament advice, *Take no thought for tomorrow.* Suppose you decide on Friday to behave in a certain way in a situation on Saturday. What makes this decision? Simply the particular desire in charge of you at the moment. But on Saturday another entirely different desire takes over, so you behave entirely differently than planned. Your desires have no power of either consistent or correct behavior, so you must not trust them. Rather, enter the Saturday situation with no preconceived ideas of what to say or do. This leaves the mind pure, unhampered and able to receive the guidance of Supermind.

By examining the point where man reverses his direction, that is, where self-defeating resistance fades and enriching self-acceptance appears, we determine that the critical turning point comes when he just can't take it any more. Sensing the secret tragedy of his life — *consciously* — he lashes out in his first rebellious attempt at escape.

Man is frustrated, as we have seen, because he has everything exactly backward. What could save him, he rejects; that which slowly destroys him, he frantically embraces. What he believes is fullness is emptiness; what he assumes is sunshine is shadow. Wherever he knocks, expecting a welcome, there is nobody home.

But our seeker for cosmic truth, in his crisis, chooses rightly for the first time. He chooses to explore *whether or not there is anything beyond his hidden horror.*

This leads to the next breakthrough. He vaguely senses

49

something entirely different from previous ideas. He hasn't the slightest idea of what it is or where it is taking him, but never mind, he is on the way.

The way is surprisingly instructive as he goes along. He sees that heroism in the Inner World is entirely different from what is called heroism in the Outer World. Inner heroism gets no applause, no medals, no name in the newspaper. No one knows about it except himself, which is all he needs. He has a new definition of heroism: in spite of all obstacles, to return to himself in cosmic completeness of living.

The advanced seeker now understands the difference between false and true greatness. If some of the men whom the world considers great were placed on a remote island with no fame, fortune or crowds, they would crack up. All truly great men attain their loftiness by separating themselves from the world, emerging only when enlightened through their own receptivity. The separation consisted not necessarily in shunning public society, but by living among men physically but not inwardly. Such cases are familiar: Christ, Buddha, Socrates, Thoreau. A certain sign of their greatness was their disinterest in collecting followers, yet their very nobility was magnetic.

More and more our sincere seeker realizes his need to do nothing except to be an aware person from moment to moment. In one flash of insight he banishes the awful compulsion to scheme, protect, avoid, revise, attack, grab, cling, retreat, resist, regret, worry, expect, struggle, insist, demand, crave, battle, blame, apologize, persuade, believe. The whole terrible burden is cleared away. In its place he has quiet awareness.

## How to Make Your Perfect Start

It is psychic and cosmic law that no man can be given anything unless he first asks for it, and asks as if he really means it. Resistance to life-liberating facts consists of a refusal to try to understand or rejecting them as items which one already understands.

When meeting spiritually cosmic ideas for the first time, you are not required to understand them. How can you? Your part is to observe with healthy curiosity and to want to know more. Such a sane and sensible approach always returns a profit.

The mind can best receive truthful ideas when presented indirectly, as evidenced by the poems of Browning, Tennyson, Wordsworth, Whitman. Their wisdom bypasses the resistance of the conditioned mind, penetrating to the intuitive self, which recognizes them as true.

So one of our first tasks is an attempt not to receive, but to remove obstacles to receptivity. Among them are negative imaginations, mechanical reactions, frozen attitudes.

Nonreceptivity to wrongness builds receptivity to rightness. Give no welcome to negative influences. Say *no* to whatever you sense is wrong for you. This is difficult at first because we do not recognize falsity. We may admire a man's dashing sophistication, not realizing that to be conspicuously sophisticated is to be probably "phony." But wisdom and strength will come. A young tree needs protection from stormy weather, but when full grown it stands steadfast against the crushing blows of the elements. Let us be receptive to the following conversation I had with one of my perceptive students:

**Q:** How can I tell whether or not I am ready to receive?

**A:** When you are first ready for a good honest cry over the whole miserable mess, then you will know. But you must weep in secret, not publicly.

**Q:** I believe I have uncovered a particular kind of resistance in myself. I get defensive when told I am wrong. Why?

**A:** It is either true you are wrong or it is not. If you unemotionally see that you are wrong, you have no problem and you don't defend. But if you realize you are wrong, but still deny it, you must then defend your shaky position. The conflict is not caused by being wrong, but by your defense of the false position. Don't be afraid to be wrong because awareness of it is the only way in the world to be right.

**Q:** But there is so much to do!

**A:** Whatever needs to be done can be done. Don't make a big deal out of it. Begin by seeing that something in you needs correction. That is your perfect start.

If you ever feel you are a problem to yourself, disregard it, as there is a sparkling something that gleams on within you in spite of yourself. Emerson declares:

*Into every intelligence there is a door which is never closed, through which the creator passes. The intellect, seeker of absolute truth, or the heart, lover of absolute good, intervenes ... and at one whisper of these high powers we awake from ineffectual struggles with this nightmare.*

*When you choose the truth, the truth chooses you.*

## Let Yourself Be Surprised by Cosmic Truth

What prevents a man from receiving that which could make everything new? The basic cause is his false sense of identity. Because he lives from imaginary pictures of being good and wise, he angrily rejects anyone who disturbs them. Socrates remarked that his listeners were ready to bite him whenever he deprived them of a *darling folly.*

An individual fails in his cosmic quest because he makes himself incapable of welcoming the very truth he seeks. He insists that truth conform to his conditioned ideas, rather than letting it be what it actually is. He is like a bee that refuses honey because the blossom is red, not blue.

Because we are self-split, we both want the truth and dislike it. A clergyman named Colerue came into contact with the powerful ideas of Dutch philosopher Baruch Spinoza. Because Spinoza's ideas contradicted his own, Colerue feared and disliked both the man and his writings. Yet, Colerue was so fascinated by the very ideas that he wrote Spinoza's biography. The confused clergyman could never understand how such an unconventional man as Spinoza could lead a personal life of such nobility.

Man bars himself from the royal life by a peculiar feature of his mind called "kundalini." This word is from the ancient Sanskrit, meaning "to think with fantastic imagination," that is, to deceive oneself. But "kundalini" is false force — no force at all. It evaporates harmlessly when its seeming slave awakens to claim his kingship.

When tempted to reject new ideas for revising yourself, ask, "How about my *present* ideas? Are *they* working out?" This serves as a shock treatment, enabling you to open the door to freshness.

Suppose you receive an invitation to live on a distant paradise island called Surprise Isle. Fascinated by the idea, you make your preparations. Since you do not know what the island is like, you consider all the things you think necessary for comfort and security. You get together lots of clothing, furniture, your automobile and so on. After long and hard preparations, you set sail.

Upon arriving, Surprise Isle is a surprise indeed. There are no roads, only lovely palm-lined paths, hence no need for an automobile. The air is so balmy and refreshing you need but the barest of clothing. You discover that all your accumulations are useless. The reality of the isle is entirely different from your imagined version. Glancing at your invitation, you see a line you missed before: *Come as you are.*

That is our problem. We do not come as we are, but as we *think* we must be. We burden ourselves with useless ideas which we carelessly take as facts. Instead of letting reality come as a new surprise, we insist that it conform to our habitual concepts and thus we spoil everything.

You and I want nothing to do with this. We want receptivity. We want to come as we are, without theory, position, power, vanity, imagination — with nothing at all. That makes everything a delightful surprise.

Here is a gem for your immediate reception (and action):

*When seen through the eyes of cosmic understanding, anything unhappy in your past is the very same as if it never happened.*

## You are Invited to an Inspired Life

The profound wisdom of the ancient philosopher Epictetus is preserved for us today because of the responsive mind of one of his disciples, a soldier named Arrian. Although both a military commander and a leader in the Roman Empire, Arrian's heart welcomed cosmic education. He sensed the magnificent message of his teacher, Epictetus, who was a former slave, and faithfully made notes. Epictetus spoke of love, life, and said, "Consider who you are. To begin with, a man ...."

There is a peculiar feature of the mind which we must understand. The conditioned mind cannot possibly value esoteric knowledge. It simply does not exist for the person living from his false self. A small child is more attracted to a shiny stone than to an unpolished diamond because he does not know the diamond's value. So it is with the unawakened man. He scorns or ignores cosmic facts. He does not know that he does not know.

Receptivity is not merely reading about esoteric ideas. It is not attending lectures, taking courses or teaching others. Many people do these things for years, yet never change a single thing in themselves. They are unconsciously trapped by the delusion that *doing* is the same as *being*. But it is not, as their daily irritation and nervousness testify.

Receptivity is something entirely different. It is an inner process that changes your values and uplifts your spirits. It is a state of mind that is beginning to love fact more than falsehood. It is a total acceptance of yourself exactly as you are at the present moment. It is a secret process, and, I might add, one of delightful charm. By its fruits will you know receptivity. You will know by what it does to you and for you. *And you will know the truth, and the truth will set you free.* (John 8:32)

The New Testament records the parable of the king who sent out cordial invitations to his son's wedding-feast. The king's servant spread the word around the countryside, but no one responded. One after another made their excuses. One man was busy with his farm, another with selling merchandise. Some of the more ungrateful ones attacked the very servants extending the invitation.

We need not look far to see the same situation today. The invitation to the inspired life is just as generous to modern men, but the resistances are just as numerous. Let's examine a few, together with penetrating replies:

But it is all so difficult.
*Do not take the difficult as the impossible.*

I already have my lifelong beliefs.
*Honestly now, what have they done for you?*

I just don't know what to do.
*Courageously abandon your fixed viewpoints.*

But esoteric ideas just don't work.
*How do you know unless you have really tried them?*

But these ideas are against having a good time.
*Are you having a good time?*

I am too deep in the pit.
*Whatever the condition you can climb out.*

I don't need anyone or anything.
*Do you say this when you are alone on your pillow?*

But I don't know where to start.
*With ruthless self-honesty.*

But *is* there something entirely new?
*You wouldn't ask unless you already sensed it.*

## How to Begin to Awaken to the Cosmic Way of Life

An anecdote from ancient days tells of two water-carriers who met on the road:

"Please," asked one, "give me water to drink."

"But," replied the other, "you have water in your bottle."

"Yes, but it makes me ill."

It is not easy to be blunt with people who insist upon retaining false ideas while expecting happiness. They must be told that the penalty for a closed mind is self-hostility and self-sorrow. There is no doubt about it. We either work against falseness and for ourselves or against ourselves and for falseness.

*Man is in a state of psychic sleep, but does not know it.*
*He can awaken to an amazingly fresh life.*

The problem and its solution cannot be stated any simpler than that.

Encourage yourself by remembering that any *detection* of negativity within you is a *positive act,* not a negative one. Awareness of your weakness and confusion makes you strong because conscious awareness is the bright light that destroys the darkness of negativity. Honest self-observation dissolves pains and pressures that formerly did their dreadful work in the darkness of unawareness. This is so important that I urge you to memorize and reflect upon the following summary: *Detection of inner negativity is not a negative act, but a courageously positive act that makes you a new person.*

One kind of negativity needs special attention. Do not feel guilty about yourself. Refuse it absolutely. Self-accusation has no place in your present day, regardless of past errors. Accept yourself exactly as you are with all your present habits. Refuse quietly, unemotionally, as if you understand that the self you accuse is a fictitious identity put together by false ideas, like a scarecrow with old and useless clothing. A scarecrow has no guilt because it is not real. There is something real in you which has no guilt.

The process of early growth into psychological maturity can be likened to a man walking through a grove of trees on a sunny day. While passing through the grove, he feels the coolness and shade of the trees. But upon stepping into a clearing, he becomes aware of the sun's warmth and brightness. And thus, as he continues to walk forward, he alternates from brightness to shade.

The sun is constant; it is only his relationship to it that changes. So does the spiritual traveler pass from gloom to cheerfulness, from doubt to understanding. But the longer he walks, the sparser the trees and the more frequent the clearings. Consider the following exchange of ideas.

**Q:** Can't we make progress merely by steady association with spiritual things? Why do you stress receptivity instead of association?

**A:** Association without receptivity is useless. A bottle of unclean water can float for years on a lake without becoming clean. For purification, the bottle must be broken. This means we must empty ourselves of wrong ideas.

**Q:** How can we go about all this?

**A:** Don't think in your usual ways. Don't talk in your familiar patterns. Don't feel the way you always feel. Don't live according to habit.

## How to Be Always of Good Cheer

Every cosmic truth has its human counterfeit. There is true happiness and false happiness, authentic progress and pseudo progress, right thinking and wrong thinking. Because cheerfulness is both good and necessary, we want to distinguish between genuine and false cheer.

Counterfeit cheer is based on a delusion. Maybe you meet someone whose exterior manner makes you feel good.

## The Power of Your Supermind

You assume he has power to help you, but a closer relationship reveals him as weak and hostile. You now see that your cheerfulness toward him was based on misunderstanding.

But there is true gaiety. It appears naturally, effortlessly, when we see things as they are. Founded on the rock of reality, it remains in place, regardless of the shifting sands of the Outer World.

The true teachers have cheerful natures. Who *wouldn't* be cheerful on the mountaintop! Such a teacher was Sri Aurobindo, who was born in India in 1872. After attending Cambridge University in England, he returned to India to engage actively in politics. He finally realized that neither a college education nor political power can develop psychic wholeness. Turning to the mystic path, he caught sight of cosmic treasure. Today the writings of Sri Aurobindo are universally appreciated for their deep insight into both the human and cosmic worlds. He combines practical instruction with bright encouragement. Here are a few cheery ideas for your daily use:

*A constant turning and returning to true life in the Inner World must result in total triumph.*

*You are created anew every moment.*

*Life becomes easy when you choose in favor of your own psychic enlightenment.*

*You perform true magic when you see what it is.*

*You need never scold yourself for mistakes in thought and speech.*

*Cheerfully follow your dim suspicion of something better.*

*Persistence along the mystic path reveals the necessary wisdom and power and opportunity.*

If you create a vase out of soft clay and do not like its shape, it need not remain as it is. The jar has no power to prevent you from changing it, as you are in charge. Its present shape has nothing to do with what you can do with it.

Likewise, your present is not fixed. The future is in your hands. You are capable of remolding everything into what you want.

The initiative is yours. Choose in favor of yourself. Do not remain a prisoner of traditions which you have been told are true. Accept nothing as true which is not *your* truth. Remember, the entire universe is on your side. If at first you awaken for only a split second out of 24 hours, you have done something marvelous. With consistent initiative, that split second will grow into a full second, then a minute, an hour, a day, and finally into endless independence.

## Special Points to Remember

1. Receptivity to cosmic truth is a great miracle worker.

2. Your cosmic growth comes by not resisting uncomfortable situations.

3. Receptivity to Supermind provides guidance, healing, comfort.

4. Be a self-aware person at all times.

5. Give no welcome to negative influences opposed to Cosmic Truths.

6. Awareness of your being wrong leads to true strength.

7. When you choose the truth, the truth chooses you.

8. Come as you are, without power, without wisdom, in constructive humility.

9. The Supermind way is the way of endless delights.

10. Be of good cheer, for all is well with your cosmic level of awareness.

# 4

## How to End Hidden Pain and Sorrow

Look within. Be watchful. Use your power of watchful attention. To illustrate, notice a television program where loud voices speak over a background of soft music. By an act of attention to the music alone, you hear it clearly, while blocking out the voices. Likewise, by watching within, there is a constant quietness, regardless of exterior noise.

*If by patience, if by watching, I can secure one new ray of light, can feel myself elevated ... shall I not watch ever?* (Henry David Thoreau)

That is what we will do together in this chapter. We will explore the problem of sorrow deeply and earnestly, watching for those liberating rays of light within ourselves.

Just as physical pain must be heeded so as to restore the health of the body, so must mental pain be used as a guide toward spiritual wholeness. Fortunately, sorrow forces us to examine what we usually prefer to ignore. When pain persists, we have an opportunity to examine ourselves anew, and so find the sure cure.

I assure you that, regardless of your particular sorrow, liberation is possible. However, you must grasp the essentials, which will be discussed in the following pages. You can awake to the radiant life, just as did Buddha. Observation and meditation upon human suffering led him to finally solve the mystery of pain for himself. The very term "Buddha" means "the awakened one." So let us explore.

## How This Miracle Happens

When troubled, we have our choice of either surface comfort or psychic understanding. If the choice is for comfort, such as associating with those who sympathize, we cannot have understanding. The demand for comfort blocks psychic insight. But if the choice is for understanding, which forces you to stand all alone without comfort, understanding breaks through. Every time we choose understanding over comfort, we walk a greater distance away from troubles, for such are caused by misunderstanding.

If you have a reason for knowing that all is well, for example, because you are financially sound or because you have family and friends, you have no genuine security. Dependency upon such things breeds fear, for you sense their impermanency. You can only know that all is well when you have absolutely no reason for it, when you have no psychological support. This is one of the seeming contradictions of the inner life which you must understand. Only when you have no support are you supported. Also, only in this free state can you fully enjoy your finances and your family, for you have no fear of loss.

The miracle happens when a person has the courage and honesty to see that he does not know what to do with himself. This is not a complicated discovery; it is very simple. You calmly and clearly see that you don't know how to run your inner life and never really did. You willingly give up the prides and vanities that insisted that all was well when it really wasn't. You can fight no longer; you are too tired and broken. With fear and trembling, you surrender your human armor and stand there ready to be slain.

61

Instead, the miracle happens. Having made room for the higher force, it now enters to do everything for you. You no longer try to live; you just let life itself live. Every area becomes new and different. Your thoughts, feelings, finances, marriage, home, friendships are all magically transformed. With great relief you now realize that the very lofty force you once feared is your only salvation. You are happy now and know that nothing can ever take it away. Take strength from the following points:

**Q:** What prevents us from doing what must be done to abolish pain?

**A:** The inability to get to the point. What is the point? The plain fact that pain exists within a man and he doesn't know what to do about it. Not knowing the right thing, he does the wrong.

**Q:** What are some of the wrong approaches?

**A:** You take the wrong approach when you refuse to see your own suffering as a fact, trying to evade it, instead of facing it. You strike out in hostility in an attempt to relieve the pressure and are unwilling to know what must be known about suffering. You pretend that all is well when all is wrong.

## The Supreme Secrets of Cosmic Powers

There is a supreme secret which few people realize: There is a power beyond human mind-power. It is the ever-present force of Reality, of Truth. Our awareness of this power makes it ours. Awareness sparks the powder trail to an explosion of consciousness.

Don't complicate your life by thinking so much about it. It is conditioned thinking, not the realities of life, that pain the heart. Habitual thinking, reasoning and rearranging do nothing for you and have never done anything for your inner contentment. Habitual thinking does you good only on the everyday level of things, like planning a vacation or reasoning out a balanced dinner. But conditioned thinking about psychological matters, like happiness and a purposeful life, cannot succeed. Mental power is limited to earthly activities, like a flightless bird.

People are actually afraid to stop pointless thinking. They are afraid to stop doing the wrong thing because they mistakenly assume that it is the only thing to do and without their frantic mental chasing, everything will fall apart. The opposite is true. When human thinking stops and spiritual awareness starts, we become unified. Attempts to use the earthbound mind to fly into spiritual skies is what makes everything crash.

Try *not* thinking about happiness and a purposeful life. Stop planning and calculating. It is possible to be happy and purposeful, but not with a hypnotized mind. The English philosopher, John Stuart Mill, believed that only the awakened mind was capable of selecting true satisfaction.

Don't be afraid to lack the answers. Don't fear being empty and uncertain. These are challenging at first, but are perfectly natural stages to pass through, like emerging from a dark tunnel into the sunlight. Stick with it. Don't demand comfort or security from anyone or anything. Abandon yourself to this tunnel which seems so dreadful, just to see what happens.

What happens is the miracle you seek. It cannot be described with words; it must be experienced personally. This is the experience you want and which you can have — reunion with your true cosmic self. Ponder the following points brought out as follows:

**Q:** There seems to be a conspiracy of silence about personal hatred. People don't like to talk about it, yet, it seems to go hand in hand with personal misery. Why is there so much hatred in people?

**A:** Hatred is a desperate attempt to protect a false sense of identity. If a man leaves a woman, she hates him because her own actual emptiness has been exposed.

Because hatred is such a fiery emotion, it supplies a false feeling of aliveness and strength. Hatred is terribly self-destructive. As the false self fades through insight, hatred disappears.

**Q:** You say that heartache is caused by not living in the freedom of the present moment. I don't understand.

**A:** It is as if you wearily dragged a heavy rock behind you on a long chain. That rock was not part of the journey to where you *now* are; it only appears that way because of the chain of memory to which you needlessly cling. Drop the chain and you experience freedom in the place where you now are, that is, in the present moment. You sometimes glimpse this freedom when half-awake in the morning, before the chain of memory attaches itself to you.

## Solving The Mystery of Suffering

Suffering of any kind means one thing: We are out of tune with cosmic harmony. As we learn to harmonize, suffering ceases.

A small child who insists upon running into the street will be spanked. He is incapable of understanding any other language. His parents spank not to deliberately hurt him, but because they love him. As the maturing child understands, the need for painful punishment ceases.

That parallels the human situation. Suffering tries to tell us of the danger of running into the streets of unreality. But stubborn little man, who always thinks he knows best, refuses the lesson and gets hurt, day after day, year after year. By studying his psychic spankings, he could grow to where they are unnecessary. The source of tears is a mind that refuses to abandon its egotistical notions about itself.

To be free of pain we must go to the very end of it. We must neither resist nor resent it. We must not be unhappy over being unhappy. Then, suffering becomes a great revelation. It enables us to see the false supports we have been leaning upon. By dropping them, the truth comes to support us completely. Everything depends upon whether or not we use our pains wisely.

The first wise action is to become consciously aware of how unhappy we are. Suffering is 99 percent unconscious in most people. They do not see the underground fire, only the volcanic explosions from time to time. Take temper as an example. A man suffers whenever he gets angry, but does he see it as pain? No, he may even take pride in it, thinking temper is a sign of strength.

I will show you how to make a definite breakthrough. Take something that distresses you, such as an annoying person in your life, a heartache of some sort, anguish over an inability to solve a problem, anything at all.

Be fully aware of it. Isolate the distress from everything else and look at it with scientific curiosity. See how it distresses you, how it makes you feel things you don't want to feel. Be conscious of what it does to you, especially how it robs you of ease.

Now, rebel against your own anguish. Do not rebel against the *seeming* cause of anguish, such as other people, but *against the very anguish within you.* This is extremely important.

Don't hesitate to declare, "I am sick and tired of enslavement to this thing. I have gone as far as I am going to go. I will not put up with it any longer. I do not need to endure it and I will not. This is the end."

Become emotional about it if you like, but do it, mean it, and it will be the beginning of the end.

Suffering must not be *escaped*, but it can be *dissolved*. So we must now explore a great error which prevents the dissolution of pain.

## How Sorrow Can End For You

Suffering humanity is like a group of people living alongside a raging river that threatens to overflow its banks. One man says, "I'll escape by staying in my home and occupying myself with my stamp collection." Another thinks, "I'll escape by getting involved in a love affair." A third believes, "The river won't get me if I go around doing good things for other people."

All miss the point. So does mankind. The flood is within. That is the only place for our attention and effort. Anything else is dangerous distraction, like looking in one direction but walking in another.

What should you do when suffering a loss of any kind, whether of spouse, friend, popularity, comfort, happiness or anything at all? The first impulse is to escape the heartache by chasing after a replacement for whatever you lost. You miss the pleasure and the sense of security it gave you. Having lost the familiar, you now seek something else you hope will become equally familiar and comforting.

This is all wrong. Sooner or later, it will leave you in even deeper despair. Even the pursuit itself is frightening. With some quiet self-observation you can detect the increased anxiety brought about by an attempt to escape anxiety.

What you then must do is really very simple, though at first it will seem difficult because it goes against all your habitual reactions to loss. You must face your new and unfamiliar situation with a sense of wonderment. Think, "How strange. Here I am, perplexed and worried. That is my state — perplexed, worried and empty. No hope, no expectations, no comfort. Well, what a new and interesting experience. I will remain with this state and not run away, in order to listen to its story."

In this state of pure wonderment, you make possible a miracle of transformation. Exterior conditions may change or they may not, but that is unimportant. The miracle does not occur in the Outer World, but in the Inner World. *You* are the miracle. And then, there is never again any such thing as loss. There is only change, which is Reality, which is happiness.

There is a special kind of suffering encountered by the man or woman who deeply wishes to snap the spell of psychic sleep. It is the "dark night of the soul" frequently mentioned in esoteric literature. It is experienced by every enlightened person, including mystics like William Blake and Meister Eckhart.

It begins when we first sense our pretensions and our emptiness. Having come consciously face to face with our own fakery, we shudder. We feel naked, alone, on the brink of disaster. This is a critical point which we must and can pass beyond. We do so simply by remaining with the emptiness and not fleeing back to our shaky shelters of external authorities, smooth words or crowded places.

It is only from our emptiness that we can learn anything new. But first we must become conscious, yes, painfully conscious of that vacancy. Pretense of fullness bars progress. But by living with the inner void, wondering at it in spite of our shudders, it fills itself by itself with new insight and peace. With that, sorrow ends.

## How to End Any Nightmares of Life

Perhaps the following question and answer discussion will assist you in understanding and eliminating problems that confront you at the present time.

**Q:** You say we must try to isolate and examine a particular pain in order to work intelligently for its disappearance. All right. I'm frustrated when I don't get what I crave. What do I do?

**A:** Let's see how craving arises in the first place. You sight an exterior object, perhaps a new car, home or maybe someone of the opposite sex. This creates a craving for possession. When you don't get it, pain attacks. Also, you picture in imagination what it would be like to have this object or person, but since it is not yours, you are torn between fancy and fact. Have you noticed this?

**Q:** Yes. You are saying that the problem resides in the craving itself, not in the attainment or non-attainment of the external object. Fair enough. So now I must ask how to get rid of burning desires.

**A:** See that they arise from a false sense of self. The imaginary self is a mass of howling cravings. All craving is a vain attempt of the false self to affirm itself and make you think it really exists. It doesn't; it is only an illusion which you must see through. No object and no person on earth can affirm a false sense of self because there is no false self to be affirmed. As long as we think there is, we chase an ever-receding illusion with all its weariness and despair.

**Q:** I wondered why you emphasized the need for observing the false self. Now I see its connection with craving, which is a terrible thing.

**A:** Craving is a cunning thief of life-force. It fools you into thinking itself necessary for your existence, while all the time it steals genuine existence.

**Q:** But what if a man attains what he craves? Doesn't that create happiness?

**A:** Let's see. Suppose he gets the new home or different spouse. His craving is only suspended in the novelty and excitement, as when you don't notice a headache when watching an exciting television show. But soon the novelty wears off. The old cravings attack once more, forcing him into another frantic search for relief, perhaps in a new object. He is caught in the vicious circle in which happiness is impossible. Please don't think I am trying to take all the fun out of life. *Are* you having fun now? I am trying to tell you of new ways that result in lasting contentment.

The devastating problem of craving can be summed up as follows: By living from a fictitious self, we are trapped by its fictitious appetites. Trying to feed such cravings is like trying to satisfy the hunger of an imaginary horse. The entire attempt is ridiculous. But as we destroy the false self, its howling appetite vanishes, just as the terror of a nightmare disappears when we awaken.

Henry David Thoreau confirms:

*When, in some dreadful and ghastly dream, we reach the moment of greatest horror, it awakes us; thereby banishing all the hideous shapes that were born of the night. And life is a dream: when the moment of greatest horror compels us to break it off, the same thing happens.*

## The Test of Your Cosmic Progress

The test of progress is not how much intellectual knowledge you have added, but how many mental illusions you have discarded. *There are those who know many things, yet are lacking in wisdom.* (Democritus)

It is painful to live from illusory pictures of who we are instead of from reality. A man picturing himself as a money-making genius will be upset by anything contradicting that picture, such as slow business. It is not really the slow business that bothers him, but the conflict between his pretentious self-image and the fact of slow business. He could be happily unaffected by all exterior conditions by being a simple, unassuming, self-unified businessman.

*If you really want things to be different, the ideas under discussion will point the way.*

Imaginary self-pictures are very cunning and the false self refuses to see them. The unnatural self never wants a man to awaken; it wants to retain him as its anxious slave.

To escape from the slavery of imaginary pictures, we must first realize that they are within us. Honest self-observation weakens their hold. As we become conscious of them, they fall away. The clink of falling chains is beautiful music.

Advancement is certain from the moment we cease to defend the false self with all its false values. The pain of defending the ego-self can be illustrated by a warrior who is told by deceitful friends that a great treasure lies hidden in a cave. No such treasure exists, but for selfish purposes, his friends wish to decoy him away. Attracted by the promise of a rich reward, the warrior leaves home to stand guard. Day and night he attacks everyone who approaches, even those wishing him well. His belief in an illusion makes him suspicious and hostile.

But as the weeks drag on, he grows weary of the strain and wonders why the promised reward never arrives. So he investigates the cave and uncovers the hoax. His awareness of his false position sets him free. He then goes wherever he wants and does what he really likes.

That is what happens to the man with courage enough to abandon imaginary values of the ego-self. He roams everywhere, tied to nothing, craving nothing, enjoying everything.

You are not your thoughts. Thoughts are but a stream flowing through your mind. You need not fight to control them. What you must do is become a passive observer of whatever passes across the theater of your mind. If you were seated in a theater, you would witness one actor after another cross the stage. If one portrayed a vicious monster, you would not really be scared. If another announced in a gloomy voice that all is doomed, you would understand that it is all an act which cannot harm you.

Do not identify yourself with troubled thoughts. Do not say, "I am scared" or "I am gloomy." Instead say, "A scene is passing through my mind, but it is not part of my true self." When you say this, you declare the Cosmic Truth. It is the truth even if you do not presently feel that it is so. See it clearly and the genuine feeling follows.

## How The Pilgrim Made Progress

John Bunyan's *Pilgrim's Progress* is both an entertaining story and a classic of spiritual and psychological insight. It tells of the adventures of Christian, who leaves everything behind to set out on the perilous journey to the Celestial City. He encounters weird people with names matching their character, like Superstition, the hypocritical Talkative, the terrifying Giant Despair. He runs into the Hill of Difficulty, Valley of Humiliation, Country of Conceit.

But the brave pilgrim makes progress. Little by little, obstacles fall behind. In spite of fears and failures, he presses onward until he reaches the Celestial City.

In this allegory, the difficulties and dangers represent psychological conditions within Christian himself. Bunyan means to show how every cosmic pilgrim must boldly set forth, conquer inner negativities, and so advance to inner light.

As an aid to our own quest of the Supermind, we can examine two of Christian's adventures.

While pausing at a riverbank, Christian and his companion, Hopeful, are downcast. The way has been rough. They yearn for an easier path. Looking around, they sight a trail parallel to a meadow. Liking its looks, Christian tries to persuade Hopeful to join him in taking it. Hopeful worriedly wonders whether it might lead them astray, but Christian confidently predicts all will be well.

Easy at first, the path becomes increasingly severe because it was the wrong one. Losing their way in a storm, they stumble about until finding shelter where they fall asleep. Next morning, more grief. They are captured by the Giant Despair and imprisoned in Doubting Castle.

Here they stop to think things over. Christian admits his foolishness at leaving the true path for what appeared to be an easy way. But now he resolves to make things right by escaping from his own folly. Finding within his clothing a key named Promise, Christian unlocks the dungeon door.

Once more, he and Hopeful set their faces toward the Celestial City.

That is the success story of every spiritual pilgrimage. Our blunders spill us into psychological dungeons, but with the key within, we escape to continue the pilgrim's progress. A second adventure occurs on Delectable Mountains. Christian and Hopeful met four wise shepherds whose names were Knowledge, Experience, Watchful and Sincere. The pilgrims were asked how they were able to make it so far, when others had failed. Pleasing answers were given and the visitors were then made welcome to stay and rest.

The following morning the pilgrims were guided to a hilltop called Clear. Supplied with a special kind of telescope, they caught a faint view of the wonders ahead. Cheered and strengthened, they exchanged farewells with the helpful shepherds and continued on their way.

Likewise will any persevering pilgrim receive rest, glimpse wonders and cheerfully walk on.

## The Source of Noble Cosmic Ideas

Lend an ear to one of my penetrating conversations with a person seeking cosmic guidance:

**Q:** Why do I get into one mess after another? Please speak bluntly.

**A:** The reason that there is no end to your troubles is because you will not face their pain with calm insight. Instead, you evade and try to escape them.

**Q:** In what way?

**A:** Watch yourself the next time you fall into a difficulty. Consider your internal reactions. You blame others, get resentful or fall into gloom. These are wrong reactions which only perpetuate the problem.

**Q:** And what is the correct response?

**A:** Simply be aware of these wrong reactions. Do not try to stop them; just be a watcher.

**Q:** But how can a mere awareness of my responses change anything?

**A:** You must discover this for yourself. I could tell you the answer, but personal experience will do far more for you.

I own a stone which appears quite ordinary to the casual glance, but to me, it is unique. It has special value over the common stones in my yard because of where it came from. I picked it up while in the army on the Pacific isle of Guam.

You too will have unique regard for certain ideas when you see where they come from — from a special place within you, from your Supermind. They are miles above ideas originating from the noisy, everyday mind, which can only substitute one confusion for another. Such ideas, originating from the secret self, are lofty, noble, honest, beneficial. They have a meaning that changes you inwardly.

Here is an esoteric idea of practical value:

People waste their lives trying to get things done for them, without strained effort on their part. There is such a way, but it comes only after personal effort of the right kind. It is like flying a kite. If you act rightly by holding the kite up to passing winds, it will naturally fly by itself. Now, life itself is our support, which means the need for finding the true life of the Supermind and not living from imitation.

*Tao-Teh-King,* the wise book of the East, comments on this. It says that when a man abides in the Way, his satisfactions are inexhaustible.

Suppose a small child wants to fly a kite, but knows nothing about natural winds. He sets the kite on the ground and tries to fly it by blowing heavily with his breath. His frustration could make him receptive to an older child's information about the wind. Then, by replacing wrong effort with right, his kite flies effortlessly.

## Cosmic Power is Always With You

What about grief caused by the foolishness of someone close to us?

Whenever a person behaves foolishly, it is useless to ask him why he did it. He doesn't know why he did it. If he did, he wouldn't have done it. He is "asleep." He cannot see his enslavement to compulsive drives and destructive obsessions. While slumbering in unawareness, he will mechanically repeat his foolishness, though with new variations. Nothing can prevent this except his own effort to snap the spell.

So once and for all, we must cease to expect good behavior from those whose psychic darkness makes it impossible. Do not expect anyone to behave better than he is able. Do not think that with a little effort he could be nicer. He cannot. He is compelled to act out the nature of his present psychic structure. If he would work with his Supermind to uplift his insight, behavior would change. But for the present, he must act as he is, just as a child of five expresses his immature age.

A *reminder*. This is what Supermind teachings are all about: With absolute clearness, we want to see a difference between our present self and the way we used to be.

Don't let errors in the Outer World turn themselves into accidents in your Inner World. Set up a psychic wall between them. Here is what this means: Suppose you make an error in driving your automobile, which almost results in a collision. Do not fall into emotional panic, getting angry, upset or nervous. Clearly analyze why it happened. Perhaps your awareness of traffic was blurred by daydreaming. Your refusal to let an outer error make you inwardly negative maintains self-command and makes you a better driver.

Following are gems of cosmic understanding wrapped in a brief conversation I had following one of my lectures.

## How to End Hidden Pain and Sorrow

**Q:** In your own work with people, what do you find to be their greatest barrier in finding newness?

**A:** One major task is to get a man to see that he does not know what he imagines he knows. So it is essential that he observe his self-deceptions and vanities. He can find newness by consistently sacrificing the pseudo-pleasure of vanity to the true pleasure of being a real person.

**Q:** Why am I so inconsistent in my efforts at self-discovery?

**A:** For one thing, because you merely seek relief from your pain, rather than total healing. The pain drives you to the doctor, but when it passes, you carelessly forget that it must attack again. Consistency comes when you get tired of the pain. When you finally discover that you are both your own pain and doctor, you can stay home and heal yourself.

Do you wish to understand all this and so make the crooked places straight? You can. Just as the power of the entire ocean is behind a single wave, so is the whole cosmic force of the universe in back of your intention to win.

## To End Hidden Pain and Sorrow

1. Liberation from all sorrow is possible in Supermind.

2. Reject surface comfort in favor of psychic insight for true serenity.

3. Do not be afraid to be without worldly answers when you rely on Supermind.

4. Never resist nor resent personal sorrow.

5. The wise use of suffering brings it to an end.

6. Anyone can awaken from the nightmare of pain.

7. Be an alert observer of the dawning cosmic ways of your mind.

8. Supermind-thinking dominates negative thinking and assures your freedom from failures.

9. You can be your own healer through Supermind.

10. The power of the cosmic universe supports your intention to win.

# 5

## How to Get Abundant Riches from Cosmic Change of Self

I can read the minds of many people who run across esoteric ideas for the first time. They say, "But I hardly know the meaning of terms like *self-awareness* and *self-observation*. I've scarcely heard of the teachers and systems you mention, such as Epictetus and Sufism. It all seems so dim and difficult."

In order to start up the Supermind trail, you need not have previous knowledge of esoteric principles. You need start only with the sincere wish to change yourself. Do not be dismayed by new ideas which seem difficult. Do not be disturbed by seeming contradictions between ideas. And especially, do not assume that what you can see is all there is. There is much more.

At the start of your quest, wisdom is a flash, not a glow.

We can recall once more the famous allegory of the prisoners in the cave, told by Plato. One prisoner dares to break out into the sunlight. He is, of course, dazed by the new brightness. This is similar to the confusion and uncertainty of anyone who decides to escape his unconscious captivity. The light of freedom is so utterly new and different that it cannot be recognized by the habitual mind. The escaping prisoner is, at first, frightened and puzzled by the change. But gradually, his psychic eyes become accustomed to the light. He sees that *this* is Reality. Previously, he assumed that darkness was the normal state, but now he knows better.

Do not try to imagine what the state of awakened awareness is like. The imaginative mind, which can only run old mental movies, cannot present the new. What we can do is to see the results of non-awareness, and go on from there. Evidence of psychic darkness is so overwhelmingly abundant that we miss it. You can find evidence very quickly. *What is bothering you at this very moment?* Whatever it is, you can awaken out of it with cosmic intelligence and the Supermind.

## How to Become a "New" You

If a violinist wishes to become a pianist, he must change his musical execution habits. If a resident of London wants to live in New York, he must change his dwelling habits. Here we have a clue to psychic success. For a spiritual desire to be fulfilled, inner ways must be changed. It cannot be fulfilled by thinking, talking or reading about change. It cannot be fulfilled by social improvements or church activities.

Self-change means just one thing — *self-change.*

*Beneficial change cannot occur through intellectual reasoning or analysis.* It cannot happen because all thought is conditioned. It can only repeat what it has been taught to repeat, based on distorted self-interest. Emerson says, *You find men talking everywhere from their memories, instead of from their understanding.* This is a great Cosmic Truth.

In the Outer World, for example, the politician forcefully declares we must change our foreign policy in order to maintain international peace, while another politician insists upon its retention. Both are foolish, for neither exterior action will change the warlike inclinations of unregenerated human nature. People always fail to consider the concealed perversity of human beings, including themselves. Nothing good can happen on the international scale unless each individual changes himself from a parroting machine to a truly spiritual person.

If you ask, "How can I change?" you find the answer in every true teaching. The wording is different, but the meaning is the same if you will seriously ponder the following human thought structures of religion and philosophy:

> Hinduism: *Discover your true self*
>
> Taoism: *Flow along with events*
>
> George Gurdjieff: *Wake up*
>
> Christian New Testament: *Be born again*
>
> Zen: *Let the mind be silent*
>
> William James: *Be genuinely practical*
>
> Krishnamurti: *Be alertly aware of yourself*
>
> Buddhism: *Abandon egotism*
>
> Soren Kierkegaard: *Be a true individualist*
>
> Mysticism: *See things as they really are*

## Two Valuable Questions to Ask Yourself

Just as the maple tree takes what it needs from earth and air to create maple sap, so can we use daily experiences to create mental newness. Whatever happens to you is the perfect teacher for learning how to take everything with quietude.

It is certain that by placing the Kingdom of Heaven first, all else is added to us. This is not an airy religious sentiment; it is more practical than a chair. We exactly place it first by *valuing* it above everything else, and most of all, above our own pretenses of wisdom. This higher evaluation comes by degrees, as we recognize the spiritual life as something entirely different from human affairs.

Sincere self-work enables you to value something truly valuable, something that endures when the excitement of worldly success fades away. You can feel it coming into your life, just as you can feel the heat of the sun, even though the sun itself is temporarily behind a cloud.

This glimpse of the new provides strength to climb even higher. Necessary knowledge comes faster. We face negativities with less timidity. Self-defeating attitudes lose their power. We make things easy for ourselves, where previously we did everything the hard way. Life becomes the great adventure it was meant to be.

*Return again and again to the two most valuable questions you can ever ask yourself:*

1. *What is my actual condition?*

2. *How can I change it?*

Regarding the actual condition, try to see yourself as you really are, not according to habitual assumptions. Perhaps through sincere self-observation you find yourself less sure of yourself than admitted. Such self-honesty radiates light.

For changing the observed condition, work with the principles of the Supermind.

## How Your "Fate" Can Be Changed

Tune in your idea of fate with the following thoughts:

**Q:** Sometimes I feel a terrifying sense of futility toward it all. Isn't that pretty awful?

**A:** It is pretty wonderful. It is absolutely necessary to consciously catch a sense of futility. Most people don't and so remain in darkness. Try to become *more* aware of the feeling without being scared of it. What an opportunity!

80

## How to Get Abundant Riches from Cosmic Change of Self

**Q:** Will you please comment on what is commonly called destiny or fate. Can we change our fate or is it fixed?

**A:** Certainly it can change. Do you really *want* it changed? That is the only question. Please do not hastily assure me of your eagerness to be different; there are great resistances which you do not see. Do you want a new destiny more than you want your old ways? You can have whichever you choose. Choose in favor of yourself.

We get exactly what we settle for, nothing more and nothing less. You attract people and events on your own psychological level. You cannot attract anything higher than your own level because you cannot recognize value above your own level.

A woman constantly finds herself mixed up with the wrong man. As long as she remains a psychologically wrong woman, she has no choice but to end up with the wrong man.

A businessman finds himself in one financial blunder after another. He must continue in his blunders until he sees their cause within himself.

If we want more quality we must first give up inferior quality, without demanding to know what the superior is like. This is the familiar Supermind principle of the vacuum. You cannot load your cupboard with real fruit until it is first cleared of wax fruit.

The trouble is, a man demands security. He insists upon a way so clearly marked that he cannot make mistakes. But the fact is that no one has ever found the way back home without suffering the humiliation of mistakes.

Swiss psychiatrist Carl Jung, a student of esoteric principles, remarked that the desire for security is the great enemy of self-discovery. Security exists, but it is not at all what the unchanged mind thinks it is. True security is a state of no security whatever, where a man's ego-self has been so demolished that the craving for safety is nonexistent. The Taoist teacher, Chuang-tse, explains, *If a man can empty himself of himself ... who can harm him?*

## The Daily Value of Cosmic Ideas

While the teachers and systems mentioned in this book have different approaches, all agree upon one point: the ability of each individual to learn a new way of living. Yes, it is a learning process, much like you might learn to speak French. But because it is an extraordinary schooling, there are special lessons to absorb.

Let's study one of the most deceitfully destructive enemies encountered along the path to the Supermind. It is the false notion that esoteric ideas are out to rob us of happiness. How often I have seen a glance of suspicion cross the face of someone in my lecture audience when given an esoteric fact. It is almost as if he protested aloud, "You are trying to take something from me!" Yes, that is right. I am trying to take the false ideas that ruin a life.

At times you may suspect that a certain idea is true, yet be unable to make it work for you. It is like watching a swimmer without being able to swim yourself. But this is cause for encouragement, not dismay. Your continued observation and practice will turn theory into action. For instance, you may sense with Emerson, *The difficulty is that we do not make a world of our own, but fall into institutions already made* .... This glimpse of something greater can lead to a remaking of your world to your own satisfaction.

Your coverage of cosmic principles may seem to be unconnected with daily events of finances, people, shopping, home life and so on. But I assure you they have every connection. They connect in a way which is presently vague, but which gradually clarifies and aids. Following is how I helped a person organize his cosmic approach:

**Q:** I try to understand, but many ideas of the Supermind elude me. I sense their deep significance, but don't know how to handle them.

**A:** Imagine yourself standing before a large painting by

a great artist. It is covered by a veil, except for a small corner. To understand the picture, you must push aside the veil. Now, every idea of the Supermind helps you remove the veil over the cosmic picture. Just learn one new idea at a time. Gradually, you will see what the canvas of life is all about.

**Q:** But isn't it enough to find a true teacher and listen to him?

**A:** Unless you have at least a grain of insight in yourself, you will not know a true teacher when you meet him. How can you recognize a pearl unless you already know what a pearl is like? After developing yourself to a certain point, you can recognize a true teacher who can speed your progress.

**Q:** What about discussing the ideas of the Supermind with others?

**A:** Here are my own rules, derived from many years of experience. Discuss the Supermind only with those who show sincere interest. Discuss in the spirit of mutual explorations, not to prove your own ideas. Never argue, but depend upon your own Supermind to enlighten you. Take a single principle and center your discussion around it. Don't wander from the point. For every minute spent in discussing with others spend an hour in self-discussion.

## How to Find True Profit in Everything You Deal With

An old Chinese legend tells of an army headed by two generals, Chon-Yu and Liang. They believed they could defeat the enemy army if only they had a fresh supply of arrows. Putting a clever plan into operation, they filled their boats with straw soldiers, including a few real drummers and buglers, and sent them toward the enemy. Hearing the sounds of drums and bugles, the enemy thought it was an attack, and showered the boats with arrows. These Chon-Yu and Liang later gathered for their own use.

And so can we use the arrows of our supposed enemies for personal profit. The stronger the attack against us, the more arrows of strength, knowledge and stability we can gather. To do so is a sure sign of Supermind-thinking.

The profit in attacks of anguish can only be seen in small ways at first. If the attack is too heavy, such as loss of someone important, we resist and see nothing. But we can take some little incident as a start, perhaps a minor disappointment or annoyance. We can see that our pain lies between what we think *should* happen and what *actually* happens. Then, if we remove the secret demand for this or that to happen, the pain-gap vanishes. We actually did not want to win the election, get the promotion or attract the praise, but really for them to tell us who we are. However, when we have no concern for who we are, we can win or lose the election and it makes no difference whatsoever.

There is a fascinating feature about the mystical life experience by everyone who has found higher ground. When he appears to lose, he really wins. Here is a man loaded with a sense of self-importance, a painful state, always calling for tense defense. As his growing honesty compels admission of vanity, it falls away, leaving temporary distress, for vanity was his support. But, of course, he has won new freedom and stability.

Following is a summary of a long conversation with a college professor.

**Q:** Why do we cling so desperately to people and objects? I see this quite clearly in myself.

**A:** Sensing change and impermanency in ourselves, we attach to people, ideas and objects in an effort to feel secure. But the effort only breeds more anxiety; it is like trying to hold back a river with bare hands. Change is a natural flow of nature. Don't fight it. Understand it. Then, everything is different.

**Q:** I admit that money-making is almost an obsession with me. If I could just resist it I could get somewhere with my inner life.

**A:** You must resist nothing. If you merely repress your desire for riches, you will never understand. Go ahead and earn all the money you want, but continue with your inner work. The time will come when money ceases to cause conflict.

**Q:** Please explain boredom.

**A:** Boredom occurs when you run out of distractions, when you have nothing to supply a false feeling of aliveness. Boredom and anxiety go together. At the same time a man seeks excitement through a contrived activity, he also senses its futility. Boredom is impossible when living from the Supermind.

## Everything from a Cosmic Viewpoint Is Truly All Right

Everyone on earth lives from one of three outlooks:

1. *Everything is all right.*

2. *Everything is all wrong.*

3. *Everything is truly all right.*

The vast majority of human beings say the first, but don't mean it. They pretend everything is all right because they simply don't know what else to do. They are all dressed up with no place to go.

A few go on to the next critical step. Unable to deceive themselves any longer, they dare to abandon their fate to the frightening unknown — a place where everything seems lost. A mystical teaching expresses it as follows: *Even as water pours into a broken ship* .... Nevertheless, such adventurers have broken through toward the shore.

Here and there, a brave individual presses on to the third step. Heeding the New Testament advice to *endure to the end* and having faced himself honestly, he finds himself fully. No longer self-split, he is One with the universe, like a single wave is part of the ocean below it. His triumph expresses itself: "Everything is truly all right."

The question may arise, "But how can I know that I am actually moving forward and not in circles?" You will know because you *sense something different going on*. There is no mistaking it. It is like sighting an obscure tree that becomes clearer and clearer as you walk toward it.

There are hundreds of hints. One of them is your greater consistency of effort. You keep on the track for longer periods of time. Moods of doubt and depression gradually decrease. Having used your insight to dissolve a small amount of anguish, you realize that greater accomplishments are just ahead. Just as a thirsty animal senses unseen water miles away, so do you sense an unseen magnificence.

Your psychic understanding develops naturally. You realize that the lower nature always tries to shove back into your day, tries to drag you down. But your understanding thwarts its deception, and you say *no*.

Have you ever noticed how intuitive knowledge comes? You read an idea in a book a half-dozen times, but then on the seventh reading, you *understand*.

When you become a new person, everything is different. What formerly seemed strong is now seen as weak; what appeared clever is now recognized as foolish; the empty becomes full; the shunned, treasured; the healthy, sick; the intelligent, stupid; the dark, light; the thrilling, dull; the friendly, hostile; the harsh, gentle.

Do not cease to work on yourself when things are going well. I have seen many people cease work, only to come running home when hurt by a playmate. If you do not work when everything is all right, you will lack the needed wisdom when life gets rough. Learn to live from your Supermind. You will be at home wherever you are.

## Change Your Inner World

People ask, "But how do I get out of this mess?" Mysticism replies, "If you were on a higher level of consciousness, you would not be in it in the first place."

True teachers rarely give advice on the conduct of external affairs. They see too deeply for that. Knowing that causes, not effects, must be altered, they try to convey this to seekers. It is pointless to advise a confused person to change or not change his employment, break off or retain a human relationship. Anything done while in psychic sleep-walking can only result in another bump against a new wall. It is really amazing how human beings can repeatedly bump for years and years without awakening from psychic sleep.

*Your inner level of consciousness or awareness determines your outer conditions. To change your Outer World, change your Inner World.*

This does not mean that every changed condition comes from a higher level of being. Changes also occur accidentally, promoted by human desire and desperation. A lonely man and a fearful woman are driven by desperation to a party, where they meet. They may get a thrill, but that is all they can get even if they marry. Loneliness and fear are still there, only now hidden by distracting each other. On the human level there is a loud shot when two people meet, but the shell is blank. On the esoteric level inner change comes first, then the outer.

Nothing is added to us when we merely change a residence, profession or spouse. It is like a man stranded on a lonely island who seeks self-betterment by moving his camp to the opposite side of the island. The scenery may be different, but he is still as stranded. We all sense this, but do not know enough about genuine deliverance in self-change.

Genuine contentment is a psychological state, never an exterior activity. If you have inner pleasure, you can engage in exterior activities and enjoy them. Without self-contentment, no matter how thrilling your worldly pursuits, heartache goes with them.

I will now slip in a special secret about external conditions that can change everything. The very next time you feel upset because you cannot command a condition, ask whether you really, honestly, actually need to have command. Mark the points in the following dialogue:

**Q:** Why am I so inconsistent in my efforts at self-change? One minute I'm excited over esoteric ideas and indifferent the next. Why all this fickleness?

**A:** You have a single desire to work on yourself and 99 desires wanting nothing to do with it. Ally yourself with the single wish to awaken and do everything to encourage it. In time there will be two energetic desires and 98 lazy ones, then three sincere desires and 97 false ones and so on.

**Q:** We read a lot about building positive images of being strong and confident. What about this idea of holding mental pictures of being strong?

**A:** It is the worst possible thing you can do for yourself. It is just an image, nothing more and nothing is accomplished, except more weakness. An aim of Supermind is to destroy, not build, imaginary ideas about yourself. Out of that emptiness can grow what is real. That reality is authentic strength.

## A Simple Plan for Your Practice

Plato advised, *Let early education be a kind of an amusement.* So, select an idea from *Supermind* and make an interesting game of it. See what you can do for yourself. Maybe you are mystified by the esoteric declaration that all human problems are caused by man's immersion in a peculiar kind of psychic sleep. Now, let this arouse the spirit of inquiry. It should! For if we are in trouble because of sleep, we can get out through awakening!

Play the game all the way to the end. Read everything you can about this strange state of mental hypnosis. Think it through. Try to understand its full meaning. Connect it with your own daily experiences. See how far you can go.

An illustration from the Outer World shows how it goes in the Inner World. In his early years, Luther Burbank wondered whether he might be able to produce a new kind of potato. He started by planting 23 seeds which he noticed on one of his potato plants. This was unusual in itself, for potatoes are usually grown from buds or eyes, rarely from seeds. As the 23 seeds grew into plants and potatoes, he ignored the inferior ones and patiently cultivated the finer results. Time after time, he discarded the small, rough potatoes in favor of the large, smooth ones. Eventually, Burbank produced the famous potato bearing his name.

Do likewise. See what you can grow from the seeds of esoteric ideas. How glad you will be that you urged yourself forward in spite of everything.

When things go wrong, look for something you do not know about the Supermind and search it out. Over the years I have found no simpler nor more helpful practice.

No matter what choices you make, do the situations get worse instead of better? *Surrender the notion that thinking from a conditioned mind can solve anything.*

Are you attacked by feelings of blame and inferiority because of unwise actions of yesterday? *Meister Eckhart remarked that if a man committed all the mistakes made since Adam, but truly turned toward the light, it would be the same as if he had never committed them.*

You have worked and studied for years and yet seen no significant betterment in your life? *Through receptivity, head knowledge must be transformed into inner experience.*

Some of the ideas about the Supermind are so vastly different from your usual beliefs that you hesitate to explore them? *Stick with them patiently, permitting revelation of their power, after which you will see them as best friends.*

You do not understand how it is possible to be in this world and yet be free of its disorder? *J. P. de Caussade compares it with a great mountain, with rain and hail at its base, while above it all, at the summit, the weather is beautiful.*

You cannot understand why you are so upset and uncertain? *It is because there are principles of the Supermind you do not as yet know and live by, but which await discovery.*

## How Self-Transformation Begins

Here is one path to beneficial change. Do not ask, "What can I get in order to be happy?" Switch to, "What can I give up in order to cease being unhappy?"

We can abandon anything ruinous, like thinking that tomorrow will be different, even though we remain inwardly the same.

We can renounce useless activities masquerading as pleasure and necessity. Henry David Thoreau made the classic remark that most men lead lives of quiet desperation. But, there are many who lead lives of noisy desperation by involvement with public affairs which do nothing for anyone.

You can cease to let others use you for their selfish purposes. If they do, it is because of self-consent. You may not allow it consciously, but because of failure to comprehend, you yield to your own harm. There is only one escape from being preyed upon and finally abandoned by weak people. You must see human nature as it actually is, not as it appears on the surface.

Suppose a farmer wishes the rain to change and refresh his vegetables. However, among the budding plants he has placed buckets of various sizes which will prevent the rain from reaching its natural destination, the earth. There is no receptivity, therefore, no change.

As we saw in Chapter 3, the magic key to self-transformation is mental receptivity to higher ideas.

Human beings live the way they *choose*, but not the

way they *want*. A vast difference lies between the two. We *choose* from our acquired beliefs, habits and taste. We select this friend or that viewpoint because they harmonize with our preconceived notions, usually false, of the best way to get along. Regardless of how often they lead us straight into grief, we don't see them as the cunning traitors they are. So we continue to stumble in our sleep.

Now, a person essentially *wants* something quite different from what he *chooses*. He wants harmony, refreshment, peace. But then he goes right ahead and assumes that his *choices* will deliver them, which they never do. His hunger remains, no matter how often he tries to fill it with the artificial foods of choice. Note how the following situation was handled:

**Q:** Will you supply a method for changing myself?

**A:** Self-transformation begins the moment you honestly place truth before desire.

**Q:** Please explain.

**A:** You desire social popularity? Face the truth that popularity is emptiness. You like to run mental movies through your mind of how someone mistreated you? See the fact of their destructiveness. You want security from a religious or philosophical doctrine? Realize that no man-made creed can save you.

**Q:** This will make me different?

**A:** Placing universal truth before personal desire sets in motion a great force in your behalf. You must place yourself aboard the airplane, after which it carries you aloft of itself.

## This Chapter in Review

1. You must start with a deep desire for self-transformation.

2. Let every experience teach you self-knowledge and cosmic awareness.

3. Make self-change the great adventure of your life.

4. By raising our psychic level of awareness, we attract new riches.

5. True security comes with rejection of conditioned thinking.

6. When living from the Supermind, boredom is impossible.

7. Everything is truly all right in cosmic consciousness.

8. When you are new with Supermind, everything appears to be different.

9. We must abandon imaginary and conditioned ideas about ourselves.

10. Place Cosmic Truth before personal desires.

# 6

# How to End
# Defeat and Failure

In this chapter we will solve the mystery of defeat and failure. Our clues come from esoteric and mystical teachings. You will find the solution as different from the usual as sky is different from earth.

Among classic legends about heroes and dragons, we have the story of Siegfried. Like most legends, it contains profound psychological insights, helpful to those who observe them.

Siegfried is called upon to slay Fafnir, the fierce dragon of Glittering Heath. Doubtful at first of his own skill, Siegfried hangs back. But true heroism finally wins out. Taking his specially forged sword and mounting his magnificent horse Greyfell, he sets out for Glittering Heath.

The journey itself is enough to shake a weaker man. At every stage there are dangerous cliffs, wild beasts, barren lands. One by one, Siegfried faces and overcomes the hazards. Finally, he comes to the crisis of his journey — the meeting with Fafnir, the dragon with fiery breath and flapping wings. It was the great moment for Siegfried and he found himself prepared, heroic. Drawing his special sword, he wins a total victory over the monster.

Siegfried's adventure parallels a stage experienced by the true traveler toward the Supermind. As we have already seen, the psychic soldier is faced by dragons of every sort. His task is to remain on the battlefield until the day is won. So we will now track down, encounter and overcome that particular dragon called failure. Like the legendary monster, the feeling of failure is a hit-and-run creature. It pops up whenever we meet a crisis in business, marriage or with an ambition. It strikes swiftly, withdraws and conceals itself, then strikes once more from an unexpected direction.

## Failure Does Not Exist

A feeling of failure is useless and unnecessary. Its exposure comes when we see that: (1) it exists within us, not in the Outer World; and (2) it has no power nor meaning in itself, only that which we carelessly give it.

Suppose I am in a haunted house which is next door to my own home. It is dark, dreary, frightening. Not liking the darkness, I beat away at it with a stick. Will that give me light? No. I must stop my useless fighting and step into the light of my own home.

So it is with failure. I will always feel lost as long as I remain in the haunted house of darkness and illusion. But when I come home, there is light and warmth.

Now, here is the idea: When I was in that haunted house, should I feel myself a failure because I could not remove the darkness by beating at it? No. Would my neighbors call me a failure? No. The word has no meaning. It was not my business to either succeed or fail in the haunted house. My only task was to get out and get home!

Do you see what we are getting at?

If you do not call an event or condition a failure, it cannot represent failure to you. This means the event or condition cannot bother you in the slightest, regardless of its worry to others. So we must find out why we call anything a failure.

## How to End Defeat and Failure

It is because we have in some way connected it with a sense of identity. We desire the event to give us money or medals so that we can picture ourselves as wealthy or famous. But all is vain. Even if we get the money or medals, we have done nothing for our true selves.

You see, man's greatest fear is the fear of being nothing. So he attaches himself to ideas of success in an effort to call himself successful. But because success, as well as failure, is a mere *idea*, he is forever doomed to disappointment. As difficult as it appears, we must abandon all imaginative ideas about ourselves. Beyond our imagination is what we truly want. When this is fully understood, life is no longer a mystery nor a misery. Francois Fénelon knew this when he wrote, *The more we give ourselves up, the more we find peace.*

Let's test all this. Think of a project in which you have no self-interest, perhaps that of becoming a scientist. Now, is either success or failure of concern to you? No. We concern ourselves with success or failure only when damaging self-interest is involved. So to be free we must abolish all harmful self-interest.

This does not mean you will not be able to earn a good living or carry on with the usual affairs of life. In fact, you will perform much better in everyday matters, for you are not concerned with failure in any way. You just do what you do, with no inner conflicts.

Strangely, when you have no harmful self-interest, you are interested in everything, but not tied to anything. You are like a ship that roams the sea, visiting whatever ports it likes and leaving whenever it pleases the fancy.

## You Can Always Find The Cosmic Awakening

Are your failures similar to those of a student who had to be handled vigorously as follows?

**Q:** I have failed somewhere along the path. My behavior is pretty awful at times.

**A:** Yes, because you are asleep but don't know it. The essential you does not consist of awful behavior; the behavior results from spiritual sleep. You must understand what it means to wake up, after which awful behavior ceases.

**Q:** Why do you emphasize the need for psychic awakening, rather than a life of action?

**A:** It is because no matter where a sleepwalker goes, he gets nowhere.

**Q:** Why don't I know I am in this peculiar state of psychic slumber?

**A:** You have not as yet worked long enough to see the difference between sleep and consciousness. If all you know is sleep, you have no way of recognizing the awakened state.

Your present way of life is not all that there is. We can rise above our habit-heavy mind to find the new, the different and the superior. The following story illustrates the point.

There was once a citizen of a country which was famous for its great apple orchards. The country's industry was founded upon apples of every color and variety. Proud of its reputation, the nation restricted itself to apples only. No other fruits were grown or imported.

One afternoon, while on a long journey to another country, this citizen became tired and hungry. Stopping off the road, he was hailed by a friendly orchardist who offered food and rest. When a tray of fresh fruit was placed before him the citizen offered his thanks, but declined the food. Then he asked, "What strange fruits are these?" His host explained, "Peaches, pears, dates, pineapples — delicious and refreshing."

The hungry citizen timidly hesitated until it became a

choice of eat or collapse. Testing the strange fruits, he found them as delicious as described. From that day forward, he no longer thought that apples were the only fruit in the world.

We must not think that the present way of life is all there is.

Step-by-step, a man now arrives at self-realization when he:

*Dimly senses something wrong with himself*

*Realizes it can no longer be ignored*

*Searches for answers*

*Encounters disappointments and frustrations*

*Gallantly persists*

*Dimly senses something new and unique within*

*Begins to change inwardly*

*Alters his external ways*

*Becomes freer and happier*

*Continues to let the truth renew him*

## The Sure Cure for Feeling Defeated

*A sense of defeat and failure can exist only when we live from unnatural ideas about who we are and what we should accomplish. When false notions melt in the light of psychic intelligence, defeat and failure disappear forever.*

Man is always chasing around trying to get credit and approval. That is one kind of false notion. If a man would cease taking credit for whatever good comes his way, he would not suffer from ego-injury whenever ill fortune arrives. When you get rid of self-credit, you also abolish self-condemnation. Credit and condemnation are a typical pair of the opposites we discussed in Chapter 2. In other words, freedom lies in rising above mere definitions of failure and

97

success, above self-approval and self-reproach. Note how the following questions were handled:

**Q:** I want people to notice me, to be attracted to anything with which I am connected. What is wrong with this kind of success?

**A:** Why do you want others to be attracted to you?

**Q:** It makes me feel good. What's wrong with that?

**A:** In other words, your source of pleasure is in the behavior of others toward you.

**Q:** Well, yes, since you put it that way. Why isn't that all right?

**A:** Don't you see that you are at the mercy of the fickleness of others? Their behavior tells you how to feel. Do you realize the slavery in this?

**Q:** But what else is there? How else can I feel good? If I give up all this, I wouldn't be able to stand the isolation and loneliness.

**A:** There will be no isolation or loneliness when you return to your original self.

**Q:** I would like that. But how do I return?

**A:** We can discuss it. Follow along.

There is a sure cure for feeling isolated and desolate. Liberation from these states also frees one from their offsprings in the form of psychosomatic illnesses.

The basic idea is not to identify with a feeling of depression, not to take it as being part of the essential self. Instead, stand aside with objective examination, just as a weather scientist might examine a dark cloud. Such a cloud would not make a scientist feel gloomy. Neither should the psychic scientist feel depressed over the observed depression.

Observe how the feeling arises, how it presses heavily for awhile, and finally fades away. Suspend personal reactions. Do not personalize by thinking, "I am depressed," but impersonalize with "A feeling is passing through."

Whenever this technique is practiced, you detach yourself from despondency to a certain degree. You weaken it. The heaviness can never return with quite the same intensity. Constant practice gives astonishing results. You can use the same method for dissolving other negative feelings, such as panic and boredom.

The mystics have practiced this idea throughout the centuries. An early mention is given by Arcesilaus, an Athenian disciple of Plato, in the following: *Suspension is accompanied by quietude.*

## How to Handle Defeat Without Despair

I will tell you of a strangely wonderful way to live. It is to live in defeat without despair. Think about this idea very attentively.

What would your day be like if you were defeated at every turn, but reacted with no despair? It would be the same as if there was no defeat, wouldn't it?

You go through your day, defeated by one event after another. You spill coffee on your clothes, the car breaks down, you feel lost, you cannot come to a necessary decision, the thrill you thought would last has faded and left you empty.

If you will let these things happen to you without reacting to them with a conditioned mind, there will be neither defeat nor despair. Both are merely reactions of the conditioned mind to an event.

Arthur Schopenhauer, whom we will meet later, explains this curiously effective technique of winning by losing as follows:

*How is inner unity even possible under such circumstances ...? To be sure, the best thing he can do is to recognize which part of him smarts most under defeat, and let it always gain the victory. This he will always be able to do by the use of his reason .... Let him resolve of his own free will to undergo the pain which the defeat of the other part*

99

*involves. This is character.*

Maybe you are unjustly accused by someone, with no way to explain. All right. You are unjustly accused. So what's the problem? There is none. You relax because you see that *the only thing in the whole wide world that can create defeat is your own belief in it.* Schopenhauer calls it *character.* It is also life-saving wisdom.

Learn what it means to live in defeat without despair. Then, no matter what happens to you, it is all right. You may not see it at the time, but it is perfectly all right. In time you will see it. Here are deep truths in question and answer form:

**Q:** I catch a glimpse of all this, but don't know what to do next.

**A:** It is quite possible for you to be in a negative state while sensing that it need not be this way. This is genuine progress. You are like a man lost at sea on a raft who sights a distant shore.

**Q:** Good. Please supply a solid idea for self-work.

**A:** Rid yourself of the false notion that things should turn out the way you desire.

**Q:** This will change things?

**A:** It will *reveal* things.

## Ten Secrets of Psychic Success

1. *Your inner essence:* Words, thoughts, actions, ambitions, convictions, all mean nothing unless they spring from that certain inner essence called the Supermind. Honey contains sugar, flavor, color, liquid, but if you mix these ingredients you will not get honey. The *essence* of honey is required.

2. *Self-unity:* The self-united man easily accomplishes that which the self-divided man finds difficult or impossible. Inner unity expands our achievements in all areas of living. We are no longer harvesters who pick one grape at a time; we take them by the bunch.

3. *Leave yourself alone:* If you do not identify with a physical defect, that is, if you do not see it as part of the essential you, it is the same as if it did not exist. Psychologically, it does not exist and, therefore, cannot bother you. So stop nagging at yourself; leave yourself alone. The reverse of the Golden Rule is equally valuable: *Do unto yourself as you would have others do unto you.*

4. *The wonderful truths:* Beyond the terrible facts about human beings reside the wonderful truths. But no man ever has or ever will find the wonderful truths without first facing the terrible facts. We find our heaven by experiencing fully and without resistance what we assume is our hell.

5. *Correcting blunders:* You can take the sting out of your mistakes by realizing that you made them because you wrongly assumed that your action was right or necessary. Operating from a false notion, you received a false effect. But now, by operating from the Supermind, everything can be different.

6. *The mystery of hope:* Never hold your hopes in reserve. Dare to exhaust them completely, the sooner the better, for they keep you tense. Have you noticed the anxiety in hope? Human hope is not comforting; it is subtle slavery. Beyond shattered hopes is what you really want. In that true life there is no need to hope. You don't hope for the sun on a bright day.

7. *How insight works:* When you *do* something because you first *see* something, your action is right. In fact, the seeing is the doing. When you solve this mystery, life will never again have a sorry sense of sameness.

8. *Avoid distractions:* Don't take side trips — that is, pay no attention to useless items, like traditions and popular opinions. It is also useless to wonder whether you can make it or not; keep trying. It is pointless to chase from one teaching to another; seek within yourself. Never mind what other people do with their lives; do what is right for you.

9. *The richer life:* The greater distance a man is from the truth, the more he will be indifferent or hostile to it, though he may give public lip service to it. The closer one is to the truth the more he welcomes it. Spiritually speaking, the rich get richer and the poor get poorer.

10. *Sailing forward:* Just as a ship sails through opposing winds by setting its sail at a certain angle, so can we, by right insight, sail through all seeming opposition. Forget opposition. Remember insight.

## Practical Wisdom from the Sufis

You show your skill as a psychic artist by doing the little things you can do, while not trying to reach too far. Perhaps you cannot break that habit, as yet, but you can investigate its mental causes. Maybe you cannot understand why you slam into one frustration after another, but you can see how labeling an event as frustrating arouses a similar feeling. You may be unable to stop self-condemnation as yet, but you can absorb *Supermind* teachings.

There is always *something* you can do, so concentrate your efforts on it. A small task, well done, qualifies you for a slightly larger success. By adding a single cup of water to a bowl of water, the entire level rises. Likewise, by making a single gain in insight, like seeing that the effortless way is surprisingly effective, you also understand other things.

As your confidence in the truth increases, your search becomes brightly exciting, like a man turned loose in a field of diamonds. You become eager to receive everything the Supermind has to offer. At this point, many students compare the teachings of all the great mystics. Surprise! Essentially, all teach the same thing: *Extend a warm welcome to the super-wisdom already existing within you.*

Sufism is a fine example of finding truth in the various religions and philosophies. The term Sufi comes from the Arabic word *sufi* meaning wool, and describes the garments of early disciples. Sufism is a mystical philosophy which arose in the tenth century and gained strength particularly in Persia and India. It emphasizes love, mental illumination, peace of spirit.

The first great Sufi was Hallaj. He was martyred when he denounced religious hypocrisy and urged man to discover the truth for themselves. Later, the mystical teaching of El Ghazzali made him a chief philosopher. But the most famous Sufi of all was the poet Omar Khayyam, whose *Rubaiyat* rises to lofty heights of beauty.

Following are typical gems from Sufi literature. A bit of comparison with thoughts from other religions will prove the basic sameness among them.

1. *Bitter things become sweet through love.*
2. *The ideal of human action is freedom from the taint of darkness.*
3. *Quit the world and be a world for yourself.*
4. *If thou art bound in chains by care for self, at once the world is as a veil to thee.*
5. *There is a treasure in every person.*

## Change Your Ideas About Success

Far above man-made ideas of success is psychic success, the only kind that counts. Psychic success is the attainment of a new kind of wisdom that produces profound changes. It is to have Supermind wisdom. It is to see: *The happiness we receive from ourselves is greater than that which we obtain from our surroundings.* (Metrodorus)

Let's take a practical example of how true understanding changes things. I select that bothersome condition known as competition. Look around. See how everyone competes with one another for friendship, romance, customers and so on. But it is ego-competition that concerns us just now, for that is a primary cause of anger and frustration.

In the Outer World, you may be in competition with others for customers for your commercial products. However, if you also live from the Inner World, you can engage freely in commercial competition without ego-competition. Because the Inner World is higher than the Outer World, you have no worry over anything, even if your competitor gets most of the business. Because the false self, which is quick to envy and resent, is out of the way, you cheerfully conduct your business, regardless of what happens.

You do not see how this can be so? Do you think this may be a pleasant but impractical dream? No, you really don't. You sense the nightmarish nonsense of tearing yourself apart mentally and emotionally, just because your competitor pulled a fast one on you.

Live from your Supermind. That is all that matters. Then, defeat, failure and competition will be as nothing to you. This is illustrated in the following:

**Q:** Why does life often seem futile and meaningless?

**A:** It seems so because of our pretense that worthless ambitions and goals have value.

**Q:** Like trying to be important?

**A:** That and also an ambition to acquire possessions and attachments to man-made organizations. It is as if a man were to mail empty packages to himself, while pretending to himself and friends that they have inner worth. His secret knowledge of their emptiness builds unconscious despair. By daring to open the packages and facing their worthlessness, he could move forward to true values.

**Q:** Please summarize esoteric teachings about failure.

**A:** Failure does not exist. You assume there is failure because you have ego-centered notions as to what constitutes success. If you drop conditioned beliefs about success, you will never again suffer from feelings of failure.

**Q:** But how can I abandon them? I crave success.

**A:** No, you crave your *ideas* about success. They are your prison cells. Society tells you that success is something at the top of the stairs. You, therefore, are sad when you find yourself at the bottom of the stairs. We must not be gullible. The steps don't exist. Man-made success or failure is nothing. You are everything.

## How to Perform Right Action

In flashes of honesty, a man sees that he hasn't the slightest idea of what to do with himself. He is in the impossible situation of feeling eager to do something but lacking any idea of what that something is. His puzzlement leads to mechanical action. In dull despair he does what he always does.

To solve the mystery, we must grasp the esoteric meaning of action, the only beneficial kind. It is totally different from harmful action, springing from distorted desires and ego-serving ambitions.

You achieve supreme insight into the true nature of things when you see that all you need to do is to let everything be done for you. This happy insight comes to the man or woman who has reached the end of his ego-self and is willing to let his true self live out its nature through him.

If you *do* anything, mistakes are made. If you do nothing, *letting your inner life happen without ego-interference,* no mistakes are made. This does not mean the surrender of anything valuable to you. It means the finding of true value. You see, the secret terror of a man is that although many things happen to him, nothing happens that is *real*. It may be new, exciting or even gratifying, but it is just not authentic to the deeper self. The more you are your real self, the less you do unreal things, and the happier you are.

How strange that people repeatedly suffer from wrong actions without questioning them. In the physical world we are very practical. If the dinner is less than tasty or if the business project goes wrong, we make examination and correction. Yet, in the inner life how few are practical!

It is not enough to sense that something is wrong. We *know* something is wrong — don't we? We must get sufficiently tired of the same old panics and boredoms to start right action. Right action starts with observation of and dropping of the false self.

You do not need to *plan* right action toward inner advancement. You need only cease wrong action which you assume is right. That makes room for action-without-conditioned-thought, which is always right. Taoism says of the enlightened man, *He does not plan, contrive or calculate.* Do *you* need to plan how the sun moves in its natural course across the sky? Believe me, it is just like that. Everything happens the way it should, when you have no preconceived ideas about what should happen.

Whenever you feel you are not getting anywhere in life, you should immediately ask yourself, "But where do I really want to go?" You will then notice the surface mind fly into frenzied action to supply you with false answers, perhaps suggesting that you want new friends or more money. But, beneath these deceptive answers is your Supermind, which sees them as false. Your task is to be aware of the false voices, which destroys them, just as sunlight dissolves dew. The time will come when you no longer fear not getting anywhere. You will see that you are already there and always have been.

You can be sure you are performing right action when you sincerely try to understand cosmic principles.

## A Fascinating Fact of Esotericism

When you step into a grocery market, you can buy as much as you have money to pay for. With a million dollars, you can wheel out the entire stock. Similarly, you can carry out of the spiritual market according to your money. What is this money? It is just the opposite of the material world. Your spiritual cash is not something you have but, strangely, something you have not. *You must come,* as the

New Testament repeats, *with nothing at all*. This is the beauty of it all.

Now we must discover the meaning of having nothing. It means to be without our intellectual opinions and memorized ideas about the inner life. In other words, we have here one of the most fascinating of all esoteric ideas: *Nothingness is richness!*

You see, knowing the words is not the same thing as living the meaning. Suppose I memorize the printed instructions on a first-aid kit. Does that mean I can give first aid? No. The full meaning comes when I admit I know nothing and then try, practice, succeed. I have known men, proud of their intelligence, who grandly announced that they had memorized entire chapters of a religious book. But, that is not intelligence. The very same men linger in a doorway for a half hour, chattering endlessly, while occasionally telling you they must leave at once.

*So we need not strain toward spirituality.* Such effort is a terrible burden. The genuinely spiritual person is one who has lost all desire to be anyone but exactly who he is, without labels and without apologies. He is what he is and that's all there is to it. Such a man is undivided, uncomplicated and contented.

In an attempt to find himself, a man may associate with religious or philosophical ideas. But this by itself accomplishes nothing. In fact it may further separate him from his real nature, for he may fall into the trap of living from fictitious mental pictures of being a spiritual or an authoritative person. He is like an actor who plays a role so long that he identifies with it; he thinks he *is* that fictitious self. You can recognize such a man by his touchiness whenever his authority is questioned.

We want to concentrate upon the single desire to be a real person. To succeed in that is to succeed in life. With this advice I have answered many queries, such as:

**Q:** But how can I help it if I fall under the avalanche of miserable feelings?

**A:** You can help it and you must. Do not surrender yourself. You can win.

**Q:** Someone very close to me is deeply antagonistic to spiritual matters. How can I get him to listen?

**A:** Heaven help you if you try! You must remember two laws. One, no one can be given what he doesn't want. Second, by attending to your own development, you will be untroubled by another's antagonism.

**Q:** What is meant by such terms as inner illumination and spiritual advancement?

**A:** Something quite simple and attainable, yet hungered after by millions. We need not complicate the definition. They mean the steady falling away of the burdens of unnaturalness, alarm, exhaustion and the addition of cheerfulness, ease, security.

## Foremost Features of Chapter 6

1. In cosmic reality, failure does not exist.

2. True success is to live from the Supermind.

3. Bring psychic awakening into your experience.

4. With psychic awakening, pain from so-called defeat fades away.

5. Non-identification with worldly conditioning produces astonishing benefits for you.

6. Never mind what others do; do what is right in Cosmic Truth for you.

7. Seek psychic success, for it alone has true and satisfying value.

8. Let your inner life flow along without ego-interference.

9. Persist in Supermind until you win authentic serenity in all situations.

# 7

# The Cosmic Wonders Within Yourself

We need not strain to know. We must, as Krishnamurti points out repeatedly, *simply be aware that we do not presently know.* The entire mission of Socrates was devoted not to teaching wisdom to men, but to urge them to see their lack of wisdom. Again and again, we must try to see the vast difference between factual knowledge and intuitive wisdom. Facts are useful for the Outer World, but wisdom serves eternity. Taoism points out, *True wisdom is different from such knowledge.*

The world needs men who are not afraid to go beyond themselves, who place cosmic wisdom before personal whims. Such a man was the noted thinker Arthur Schopenhauer.

For many years, Schopenhauer roamed about his native Germany, probing the secrets of life in libraries, universities and in life itself. Coming upon the literature of the East, he was amazed and delighted at its similarity to Western religion and psychology. Still, second-hand information was not enough for the daring Schopenhauer. He determined to suspend all his adopted ideas and to think for himself.

## The Cosmic Wonders within Yourself

So settling down to a quiet life at Frankfurt-on-the-Main, he enthusiastically plunged into the mysteries of man.

Years passed and Schopenhauer changed. He became a new man. The Supermind took over. Like La Rochefoucauld, Erasmus and Nietzsche, Schopenhauer saw human nature as it really is, not as self-deceived idealists like to picture it. Did his insight mean he was a pessimist? Not at all. Like all awakened men, Schopenhauer knew that humanity must first see itself as ill if it is to find the cure.

The enlightened Schopenhauer set down his findings with refreshing directness and clarity, as the following selections of his understanding indicate.

1. *There is one thing that, more than any other, throws people absolutely off their balance — the thought that you are dependent upon them. This is sure to produce an insolent and domineering manner towards you .... The only way to attain superiority in dealing with men is to let it be seen that you are independent of them.*

2. *Your friends will tell you that they are sincere; your enemies are really so. Let your enemies' censure be like a bitter medicine, to be used as a means of self-knowledge.*

3. *Himself is the source of the best and most a man can be or achieve. The more this is so — the more a man finds his sources of pleasure in himself — the happier he will be .... For all other sources of happiness are in their nature most uncertain ....*

4. *He who can see truly in the midst of a general infatuation is like a man whose watch keeps good time, when all the clocks in the town in which he lives are wrong. He alone knows the right time ....*

## Your Source of True Cosmic Aid

Every man and woman senses that there is something else besides his usual routines in business and home. He may not know what it is and may have no idea of what to do with it, but still he knows. His dim awareness of the difference between this voice of promise and his present emptiness keeps him in despair. He is like a man who wants to go home but has forgotten the way.

Man's frustration can be tracked back in every case to compromise with his original nature. He fails to obey *himself*. *Whatever cannot obey itself is commanded. Such is the nature of living things ....* (Nietzsche)

You know what is right. Deep down, you know. The battle between your true wisdom and the counterfeit wisdom of society is what causes frustration. Refuse to compromise with what you know is right — *with what is right for you.*

Suppose a man is given a phonograph record with pleasant music on one side and screeches on the other. Playing the record over and over, he cannot understand why he gets discord instead of music. He plays the wrong side, but doesn't see his mistake. Likewise, we have music in our hands right now, but unthinkingly play the screeches.

Maybe the man with the record gets tired of all that noise. What is he to do? Well, he has two choices. He can personally experiment with the record until he sees his mistake. That is what we can do when weary of a screeching life. *Let us put the ideas of our mind, just as we put things of the laboratory, to the test of experience.* (John Locke)

The other choice can be to ask other people for advice. Now he is really in for it. Others, flattered by being asked, always give an answer — always wrong. They play the wrong side themselves.

This brings us to the question: Who is qualified to help a man make the great experiment? Clearly, it is the man who has already heard the music for himself. There are such men and you have met some of them in this book.

I have anticipated some of your questions on this score as follows:

**Q:** If true teachers are available, why doesn't everyone listen to them?

**A:** Did everyone listen to Christ, Plato or Spinoza? Or did they only give lip service to their teachings?

**Q:** Why are such men often scorned?

**A:** The ego-self always scorns anyone who threatens its false power. Remember, no man can see above his own head. A true teacher has esoteric knowledge, but unless you also sense it, it does not exist for you. Therefore, you will not value the true teacher. To the contrary, you will avoid him.

**Q:** If I avoid the true, then I must gullibly follow the untrue. I suppose this is what is meant by false prophets.

**A:** Yes, it is mutual deception. A false prophet is like a schemer who passes off an imitation painting as a rare masterpiece, while getting paid in counterfeit money.

**Q:** What a strange predicament we human beings are in!

**A:** It is needlessly tragic. The more advanced the true teacher, the less he appeals to the masses who don't want the riches he offers, yet the more valuable he is to the few who do. Be one of the few!

## Case of the Bird with the Golden Plumage

From the religious philosophy of Vedanta comes a fascinating parable revealing the majesty of man.

Two birds perch in the same tree, one on a top branch, the other on a low one. The bird on the upper branch sits in quiet and peaceful contemplation of all that goes on around him. Reflecting his golden plumage, he rests in majestic splendor.

The lower bird hops nervously from one branch to another, sampling the fruit. Coming across sweet fruit, he chirps excitedly; chancing upon sour fruit, he falls into disgusted depression. Glancing up from time to time, the lower bird is vaguely impressed by the magnificent manner of the upper bird. The nervous bird longs to know the secret serenity of the other, but soon forgets his yearning when sight of new fruit attracts his attention.

So back and forth, up and down, hops the lower bird, switching every few minutes from sweet fruit to sour, from elation to disappointment, from smiles to tears. Seeking sweet fruit only, he despairingly realizes that the sweet is always followed by the bitter. No matter what he does, sour follows sweet. He glances hopefully upward at the peaceful bird, but compulsively returns to his frantic searchings.

The time comes, however, when the lower bird gets a mouthful of fruit so bitter that he can no longer take it. The crisis is here. He must choose something entirely different or lose his sanity. So he hesitantly hops upward toward the peaceful bird, coming closer and closer.

At a certain point in his timid approach, a miracle occurs. The lower bird realizes that *he* was the upper bird all along! He simply did not see it. In his illusion, he thought there were two separate birds, but now knows that only one exists — his unified self.

Now perceiving that his frantic hoppings were done in hypnotic illusion, now knowing that he himself is the majestic bird, he is above both excitement and grief. He no longer seeks happiness outside himself; his true self is happiness itself!

This story contains a wealth of esoteric gems for your personal use, which are as follows:

1. If you don't like your life as it is, you can change it.

2. *Above the opposites of human sorrow and happiness is Happiness; above anxiety and peace is Peace; above evil and good is Good.*

3. No matter what your present difficulty may be, someone else has been healed of it and so can you be healed.

4. *Let it be a source of strength and comfort that you are never without the urge to find the way upward, back to your original self.*

5. You have made a major breakthrough when you realize, even vaguely, that something beyond your ordinary life actually exists.

## The One Way to Feel Secure

Let me set the stage for you on this matter of security as follows:

**Q:** I feel insecure. No matter what I do, it returns to haunt me. Please discuss this problem.

**A:** Security cannot exist *because* of something. If it has a cause, that cause will sooner or later change, pulling the platform out from beneath your shoes. Security is when you have no security whatsoever, no attachments, nothing which to cling to.

**Q:** Does that mean I will drift aimlessly!

**A:** Do you understand what happens by using the phrase *drifting aimlessly*? You have made yourself afraid of non-attachment by slapping on it a label loaded with negative associations. Do not label the state; rather, let it reveal itself to you as it actually is.

**Q:** Does this apply to the security we seek in ideas and ideals about ourselves?

**A:** Very much. You must not seek security by calling yourself this or that kind of person. It is meaningless.

**Q:** But I want to know who I am!

**A:** With earnest work, that problem clears itself.

Do not be afraid to be uncertain. Uncertainty, patiently endured, leads to certainty. Here is a great mystery. When you can be uncertain and not demand certainty, when you do not force things to happen in a way you assume will relieve your pressure, when you are perfectly comfortable

115

with your uncertainty, you are secure. But now, that word has an entirely different meaning.

Augustine, whose writings reveal many secrets of the universe, made a classic remark about this. He said that if anything was certain, it was his own uncertain state of mind. To know that you do not know is the dawn of knowing.

How can the wisdom of not knowing be achieved? You must have the courage to ask, "What would happen to me if I stopped running?" Then, find out. Stop running. You will see something. What a relief to stop running.

From the *Gulistan*, or *Rose Garden*, a book of ancient Persian wisdom by Saadi, comes this story:

A dervish who owned little of the world's material goods reflected to himself, "How much easier it is to live in simplicity than to be obligated to those who might enrich me."

Someone told him, "Why remain as you are? There is a wealthy man in town who delights in helping worthy men such as you. If he becomes aware of your needs, he will surely supply you."

The dervish replied, "Hush! I am happy as I am. It is folly to plead for anything from anyone."

You can own the entire world, but your ownership comes when you don't care whether you own it or not. If you are compelled to own the world or any small part of it, your desire is an attempt to feel secure through possession. But there is no security in possession, but just the opposite — anxiety. When you have nothing, you have everything.

## Here is Your Magnificent View

From my previous book *The Mystic Path to Cosmic Power* (West Nyack, N.Y.: Parker Publishing Company, Inc., 1967) comes this illustration:

*Mankind can be likened to a large party of tourists searching for a new homesite. They board a train that can take them from a dry and dreary desert to a grand and lofty mountain top. The travel guide assures them that the higher they go, the greater their capacity to see and enjoy the countryside.*

*There are station stops all along the upward way. A tourist may get off and end his trip at any point he likes. He is perfectly free to cut himself short or to continue all the way to the top.*

*Some get off at the first stop. They find themselves in desolate country. They settle down in secret despair.*

*Others go on for another station or two, then take their leave of the train. Their location is somewhat better, but still they settle down with a vague uneasiness.*

*A few others, the enduring ones, keep going. Somewhere along the early part of the journey, they made a fascinating discovery: Though the trip certainly has its challenges, the further they go the easier it becomes. Patience and persistence present sure rewards. So they eagerly press on. As they do so, they reach the peaks of happy and unworried living. With enormous relief they find that the mountain top was not just something announced in the travel guide; it is real, it is there, it is theirs.*

Think of your studies of *Supermind* as an upward journey to new levels of pleasant understandings. Do not cut your trip short by abandoning the train at lower levels. Some seekers do this whenever they encounter esoteric facts which are contrary to their habitual notions. But, if you want the peaks already prepared for you, let the facts offer a new look at life. They may be startling at first, but change magically into a magnificent view.

Here is a startling fact: Unless we are right within ourselves, we cannot really enjoy the exterior world of nature and social activities. *We can only use them as distractions from our secret sorrows.* But, when we are one with ourselves, we are one with everything. There are no conflicting divisions between the Inner World and the Outer World. Then, daily activities are pleasant, easy, rewarding.

Now, can you take this idea and see how it applies to you

in a very personal way? Can you plunge beyond the words to see the fact? If so, you are becoming a psychic artist. And that is what leads upward to a new level. That, in turn, is what liberates you from whatever bothers you.

## The Magic of Self-Awareness

Awareness can do the following for you:

1. Dissolve dangerous illusions
2. Snap the spell of psychic hypnosis
3. Enable you to see things as they are
4. Destroy the painful false self
5. Deliver lasting happiness

We want to inquire into this idea of *awareness*, for it is a major pillar supporting a first-class life.

The definition of awareness is very simple. It means that we stand aside and watch everything happening to us, both within and without. We are quiet observers of thoughts, feelings, conversations, our own facial expressions and those of others, of attitudes, beliefs, of noting the manner in which we walk and how we react when surprised.

Now, it is essential that we do not assume that we already are self-aware persons. Everyone thinks he is! But awareness is much deeper than we think so we must assume nothing about it. Rather, we experiment.

Start by being aware of the Outer World, for this is the easiest. Notice someone nervously drumming his fingers on a table or gesturing while talking. Notice that he is unaware of his movements. Now, observe your own physical actions. Sooner or later, you will see that you were unaware of these mechanical movements. That is a fine start.

Now go on to internal mechanicalness. Watch how feelings of irritation arise when someone criticizes you. Observe the wave of depression aroused by hearing bad news. This makes you acquainted with yourself.

One benefit of honest self-observation is awareness of inner contradictions. A man who insists that he is happy discovers he has been kidding himself. Ordinarily, we fail to see contradictions, for no one can see what he is unwilling to see. It is like the man who declared, "I am not always right, but I am never wrong." Self-study breaks down the walls between reality and illusion, thus making us whole.

In your first experiments with self-awareness, do not select a major difficulty. Watch for minor disappointments and annoyances. Become aware that you are disappointed or annoyed, and stop right there. Do not wrestle with these little foxes. Quietly watch as they appear, pass and disappear.

You see, consciousness is like light. The more light you have, the better you operate, just as a gardener is more skillful during the day than at night. You can see what you are doing.

You will recall our previous points about mental movies. Here is a great place to snap self-hypnosis and become a self-directed man or woman. Whenever you catch a horror movie running through your mind, when you find yourself repeating nagging thoughts, shake them off at once. Refuse to be dragged along by the spell. In its place, be aware of where you are and what you are doing, for example, walking down a hall. *Every time you do this you weaken self-hypnosis and strengthen self-command.*

*You have a choice of either life or Life.*

*The magic of self-awareness leads to Life.*

## How to Be Shockproof in Any Situation

Could this be magic? If you don't mind facing your confusion, if you don't seek protection from it with borrowed theories, it is the same as if the confusion did not exist at all! This is true magic.

Whenever confused about anything, you must place awareness of your confusion first. By doing this you create a healthy shock within yourself. It is a shock because it cracks the fixed habits of conditioned thinking which loudly insists upon contriving a way out. But the conditioned mind is in utter darkness about the way out. Awareness is healthy because it sets into motion the power and clarity of the Supermind.

Try to see the difference between mere mental improvement and the development of cosmic consciousness. Mental improvement is good and legitimate, as when learning a profession or sharpening your skill at chess. However, mental improvement cannot penetrate the psychic world to make you happier, freer or intelligent in the cosmic sense. To store facts away in the memory is like feeding information to a mechanical computer. The computer can only repeat what it has been told and nothing more. But consciousness — awareness — is always something new. It is never the mechanical parroting of memorized information.

We do not *use* the Supermind, as if it were one thing and we another. As mystics have proclaimed throughout the ages, *man and Cosmic Intelligence are One.* In essence, a man *is* his Supermind. Your aim is to be one with yourself.

The following is for constructive help:

**Q:** I am so often shocked or disappointed at what happens to me.

**A:** The happening itself is shockless. What causes shock is the expectation that something else *should* have happened. When we don't demand that happenings conform to our desires, we are shockproof.

**Q:** The way you simplify things is of great aid to me. So please tell me, in summary, what causes mental pain?

**A:** Pain occurs when reality breaks off your mental dream, like the annoyance you feel when deeply interested in a television movie and the film breaks.

**Q:** I sometimes feel that I have gone as far as I can.

**A:** Never assume you have reached the end of your

successes, any more than you would believe that a major highway ends at a small town it passes through.

## The Truth about Cosmic Love

Like other cosmic virtues, love has its human counterfeit. No artificiality is more heartbreaking than pseudo-love, whether given or received.

True love is the natural state of man and the universe. An unnatural man is therefore incapable of it. Only a conscious person is capable of love, for it blossoms only with the absence of unconscious hostility. To find true love we must voluntarily give up what we like to *call* love.

Love is not the trading of mutual benefits, it is not sentimental emotions, it is not unconscious imitation of those who seem loving. Sufism instructs, *Love is not to be learned from men.* It is much higher than men.

Love is not the assuming of an attitude one thinks he *must* or *should* have. That is only an attitude and nothing more. Love never *must* do anything for anyone. If there is a sense of duty, it is not love, but self-centered compulsion.

A relationship begins between two people when they receive or hope to receive some kind of reward from each other. The relationship ends when the reward ceases to be given or when they think a greater reward can be gained elsewhere. This is human relationship, but it is not love.

If we truly love another person, we will not seek merely to relieve his suffering with comforting words or acts. Rather, we will let him face his crisis, not interfering with the lesson, but aiding him to understand it. This often appears to be indifference, but it is love blended with wisdom.

Blaise Pascal seemed to have behaved harshly toward his sister Gilberte. It was compassion. He cared too much to permit her to become harmfully attached to him. This is typical of those who see deeply, including Christ. Regardless of the consequences to themselves, they gently push away those whose growth requires self-reliance.

You are living from the Supermind when you are able to say *no* to weak people without rejecting them. You say *no* because your integrity demands it; you simply cannot approve of their behavior. Realizing that they are bad only because they are asleep, you say *no* to them and love them at the same time. This requires genuine courage, especially when the other person is close to you. *For this is the hardest of all: to close the open hand out of love ....* (Nietzsche)

Love does not insist upon a permanent object for itself. To claim a permanent object indicates insecurity, dependency, hope for returned rewards and perhaps unconscious hero-worship. Love has none of these. It asks for nothing in particular upon which to shine. It just shines.

Love just *is*. When we see this, we no longer seek someone to love or someone to love us. We just love and that is all there is to it.

## A Fascinating Experiment in Psychic Awareness

A student once asked me, "I find it hard to believe that I live in a state of psychic hypnosis, as you teach. I think I am a perfectly conscious individual."

My answer was as follows: "A simple experiment will prove two facts to you — that hypnosis is a fact for mankind — that you can awaken from it. The next time you are alone, become alertly aware of yourself. Be conscious of your body, surroundings, thoughts and feelings. As Gurdjieff would say, *remember yourself.* An hour later, be aware of yourself again. Once more, be conscious of everything outside and inside you. You will make a startling discovery. During the interval between your two periods of awareness, you were in a state of psychic sleep; *you did not know that you existed.* The interval passed without you being consciously within it."

The reader can experiment for himself right now. Pause in your reading of this book to be aware of yourself as outlined in the previous paragraphs. An hour later, awaken

122

to yourself again. Do this until you get it. Nothing will surprise you more or be more beneficial.

A wandering minstrel came one evening to the castle of a Danish king. After entertaining the monarch and his royal court, he was given dinner and a room in which to sleep for the night. Because it was a bit chilly, the minstrel wandered around the castle in search of an extra blanket. He happened to enter the king's bedroom, and since it was unoccupied, he strolled around in enjoyment of the warmth and luxury.

He sat on the king's bed. Then, becoming bolder, he fell asleep. A few minutes later the king entered. Finding the minstrel on his bed, the king ordered the intruder out into the night. The minstrel nodded and asked the angry king, "Would you like a few words of philosophy before I leave?" Astonished at the question, the king nodded.

Said the minstrel, "I was asleep for but a few minutes, which cost me the comfort of your castle. But you have been asleep for years, which has cost you a comfort which you cannot imagine. Do you know what you have paid for your sleep? I will return to my freedom outside these walls. But you, unless you cease to sleep, will remain a captive of yourself."

## How You Can Discover Cosmic Wonders

A frightened mind invents gods which it hopes will relieve its fears. It invents religious gods, human heroes, gods in the form of worldly success and artistic achievements, but all is vain. Such tricks cannot fool the man. He detects the trickery of worshipping the projections of his own frightened mind. But still he sets up his idols. It is as if a man who feared robbers were to draw a large picture of a policeman and then hold imaginary conversations with it about his safety.

Arthur Schopenhauer put his finger on the problem when he wrote, *Hardly one in ten thousand will have the*

*strength of mind to ask himself seriously and earnestly —*
*is that true?*

But there is a way out. We can become aware of all our nerve-wracking pursuits. We can see how they distract us from finding the true self. If we discover a mental noise to be of our own making, that very discovery is a step to quietness. If noise comes from the blaring Outer World, we can gradually cease to listen. Fresh strength surges through you every time you become quietly aware of yourself. With silent receptivity, all things are possible.

Growing consciousness is like peering down a dark well with a series of flashlights, each one more powerful than the last, until at last we see everything down there. That is the beginning of the end of unconscious self-destruction. For example, it is terribly damaging to be angry, while unaware of it.

Whenever a person insists that he does not have a particular negativity, perhaps pride or resentment, he should always add, "That is, I have none *of which I am aware.*" This helps him in two ways: It makes him more honest, and it starts the healthy train of awareness of his hidden features. From that point, he can ride to freedom from their unseen hold upon him.

This false mind capable of so much grief is called by Vivekananda, the Vedanta teacher, *the traitor mind.* Our task is to understand the false ways of this traitor within our ranks.

How can we do this? Through cosmic understanding, as follows:

Self-study and self-knowledge are the great revealers of everything in the cosmic and physical worlds. When you truly know yourself, you know everything necessary to know. You know why you are dissatisfied and how to change things. You understand why war occurs, and the only way to peace. The secrets of human behavior in all situations are open to you. You know why counterfeit love often appears warm and comforting, while authentic love seems to be cold and distant. You perceive why you have faltered in life, and you are now in command of correction.

Don't try to be happy. People do this all week long and nothing happens. Instead, work at understanding yourself. That is what works.

Remember, you don't have to know everything in order to progress. You need only be on the right track of things. By your willingness to receive, even as you read these lines, you become more right, in an entirely new way.

## Helpful Points to Think About

1. Make it your aim to go beyond your worldly self.

2. Follow the unfailing wisdom of your Supermind.

3. If you don't like your life, you can change it for the better.

4. Let your Supermind-studies be a pleasant and satisfactory journey.

5. Self-awareness in Cosmic Truth delivers permanent happiness for you.

6. Practice sincere self-observation daily and faithfully.

7. As cosmic self-insight comes, painful confusion goes.

8. True love in Supermind is the natural state of man.

9. With psychic self-enlightenment, all good things are possible.

# 8

## How to Make Your Human Relations a Pleasure

When man fails to get on, it is usually because he is looking for solutions that don't exist. Nowhere is this more evident than in his human relations. His mind is like a hard chunk of ice floating down the river, constantly colliding with other chunks. Plato points out that correct principles of human relations are based in cosmic science. As long as man insists upon his own shallow rules, people will bump into people.

But all can be different. We can learn cosmic science. We can react rightly or wrongly to unpleasant contacts with people. *Here is the Supermind way for success:*

1. *Stand aside from yourself and watch your reactions.*

2. *Don't resist, condemn or seek to change the reaction, but quietly watch it come and go.*

Maybe you hear bad news. All right. Watch how painful thoughts and feelings grab you in an uncomfortable squeeze. That is all you do, merely watch, be aware. Don't call them your own thoughts, for they are not. They are foreign intruders who seek to force themselves upon you.

They have no real power whatsoever.

Repeat the two steps every time unpleasantness occurs. In time, an astonishing change will take place within you. You will see things differently. Exterior events will lose their ability to hurt, frighten or puzzle. You will realize that unpleasantness is not something to fight, only something to understand.

## How to Be In Command

Nothing builds inner strength faster than the simple practice of taking full responsibility for your reactions to whatever happens. This includes your reactions to new ideas you meet in *Supermind*.

What can you command? You are in command of everything that is below your own psychic level. If you are above cruelty in yourself, you cannot be commanded by the cruelty of others. If your level is higher than hysteria, you are immune to the mass hysteria of mankind, expressing itself in fighting and deceit.

What commands you? You are commanded by anything above your own psychic level. This is why a man on a low level of esoteric understanding has problems with both himself and other people. His various conflicts are above him, out of reach of his handling, like storm clouds.

If you feel yourself commanded by people and events, set yourself at ease. Remember the one item that is always subject to your possible control — your own clarified mind. *Your mind can control everything because of its supreme power to react correctly to everything.* In the Outer World people may seem to exert command over you, as with unjust taxes, but no one can control your mental reactions to outer events. Nothing in the Outer World can touch a man living fully from his Inner World.

A situation becomes what the mind calls it. But what happens if the conditioned mind refuses to call it either good or bad? What then happens? Well, a kind of miracle.

It becomes simply a neutral event without power to harm or to give temporary excitement, followed by the inevitable swing over to gloom.

You grow into true command as you uplift your level of being through more insight, by extending a warm welcome to esoteric facts, and especially by extinguishing a false sense of identity.

Add daily to your stock of information by going over the principles of *Supermind*. Before performing any task, we must learn the nature of the task. Learn what you must do. Your information can then change into victory.

## How to Avoid Errors with People

People are not what they seem. There is as much difference between their exterior and interior states as there is between the inner and outer sides of a house. Whenever you meet someone for the first time, you can be absolutely sure that he is totally different from what you think he is.

The mistake is our own false assumptions. For instance, we assume that a certain person is the calm type. We have made two mistakes. First, we do not see the emotional turmoil he suppresses when in public view. Second, at the moment of our observation, there is no particular crisis to arouse and reveal his panic. Surface calm will explode sooner or later, as many a bride or bridegroom discovers too late.

Our task is to see people as they are, not as we want or need to see them. Then, we make no mistakes.

How can we do this? Since other people are invisible, psychologically speaking, how can we see them as they actually are?

This can be accomplished by understanding ourselves. When you frankly face your own motives, you see the motives of others. By understanding your own desires and actions, you understand why others act as they do. Self-knowledge is the unlocking key to insight into others. Perhaps, in a moment of intense self-honesty, a man sees in himself a selfish motive masquerading as generosity. Not only is he healthier and happier than before, but he can no longer be tricked by others with the same masquerade.

It works both ways. You understand other people as you understand yourself. As you win insight into your own actions, the behavior of others becomes clear.

Whatever happens to you in social relations is quite valuable, providing you let it shed light about yourself to yourself. Human encounters are beneficial challenges to our fixed ideas. The best challenges are those revealing us to be less noble than we assumed, for the shattering of imaginary ideals is the shattering of unseen chains.

Just as we become acquainted with our nature through self-observation, we can learn about the other man by watching him in daily action. We should not do this out of mere curiosity, nor from a critical viewpoint, but because we want the facts about human nature.

Watch, for instance, how a man behaves when accused of something. Whether the accusation is accurate or not, notice whether it arouses anger, indignation or accusation in return. The ego-less man, the man thinking from his Supermind, has nothing to defend, therefore, cannot be upset. But a lesser man, with a gulf between himself and his Supermind, will react offensively and defensively.

Arthur Schopenhauer supplies another test:

*A man shows his character just in the way in which he deals with trifles — for then he is off his guard. This will often afford a good opportunity of observing the boundless egoism of man's nature and his total lack of consideration for others; and if these defects show themselves in small things or merely in his general demeanor, you will find that they also underlie his action in matters of importance, although he may disguise the fact .... Do not trust him beyond your door.*

## Be Independent of Others

By steady self-observation, we can see the difference between living from society's subtle demands and from our own center. Any discomfort we feel is trying to show us the difference.

Plead for nothing. Chase no one. Refuse to trade yourself. Stay right where you are. Do not be like a man sitting in his own living room and thinking, "I must hurry home." You are home right now, right where you are, whether in factory or field. You are with yourself. And that is all — if you see it — that you need.

We must be able to take or leave people before we can take them beneficially. A compulsive need for society indicates lack of self-command, which means placing ourselves at the mercy of others in order to get what we assume we need. And, if we ever find a man who will not in some subtle way take advantage of this human weakness, we have found one man in a million.

Never deal with a neurotic or an unpleasant person on his terms. Deal with him on your terms or not at all. This means you break the relationship as far as the Inner World is concerned, even though it continues in the Outer World. Never sacrifice your inner integrity to anyone, anytime, anywhere. Note the following truths I told my questioner as follows:

**Q:** Why am I so ill at ease with people?

**A:** This is so because you behave to please them, rather than to please yourself. This pleasing of others is based in anxiety. You try to please them because you want certain benefits, but fear you won't get them. What are some of the things that people want from people?

**Q:** Oh, it's an endless list. Money, sex, friendship, approval, praise, acceptance, security. But is it wrong to want these things?

**A:** It is wrong to surrender yourself in order to get them.

Such self-sacrifice breeds self-dislike, producing pain and hostility. Try to see the agony of living under the psychic domination of another. Notice the anxiety of waiting for another's approval or letter or appearance. You don't want to live like that. There is something entirely different.

Francois Fénelon showed sharp insight into the human situation by asking, *What do you not have to suffer to keep the respect of those men you dislike?*

The realization must come that many of your friendships are no friendships at all. You must see how you are trading your inner treasure for breakable toys. With such realization, you will no longer give what others cunningly demand of you. Then, they will leave you. They always do. Having drained you of all they can get, they depart.

Your task is to bravely bear the temporary shakiness arising from your aloneness. Be patient and have no regrets. You have done the right and necessary thing. Every abandonment of a crutch brings shakiness at first. All is well. Remain quietly with your aloneness until it tells you its supreme secret. It will.

## Why Friendships Fail

No human being on earth has power to do anything for you or against you. If you can see the significance of this, your relations with spouse, friend and stranger undergo bright transformation. You will never seek to influence others, you will never worry whether they like you or not, you will be at peace with everyone, even though they are not at peace with you. But this must be seen with the spiritual mind, the Supermind, not with human logic or conditioned reasoning.

We prefer believing in the ability of others to help us because of our desires toward them. But this arouses friction, for others have desires contrary to our own. A desire toward another creates an unconscious insistence that the other *should* and *must* behave the way we wish. When he does not, we feel cheated, resentful. We falsely think the wound came from the other person's selfishness, when in fact, it came from our false desire. When we no longer have false desire, painful disappointments are no longer possible.

Whatever the human relationship, you must not form a psychological attachment to the other person. You must freely let him come and go as he pleases. You must not try to hold him or her to you. Even if you hold him physically, his heart will be far away, which you will painfully sense. When living from your Supermind, the continuance or ending of a relationship does not depend upon you, but on the other person. This means you are free.

Remain psychologically detached from everyone. This means *everyone*. No, this is not cold indifference; it is something extraordinarily warm — it is genuine love. If you will do this, everything changes. It changes because you make no conscious or unconscious demands upon another. Strangely enough, you are in charge of the relationship because you have no charge at all.

The reason why so many marriages and friendships fall apart is because each party tries to receive what the other cannot give. Two people meet. They thrill at the newness and novelty of the other. When the excitement passes, as it always does, emptiness is seen. Then comes the despair and the seeking in a new direction. And so the vicious circle whirls endlessly.

The seeker fails to realize the futility of finding in another what must be discovered in himself. Even if a sad and lonely person were to meet someone with a lofty love, the seeker could neither recognize nor appreciate it. We can recognize true love in another only when we have at least a taste of it in ourselves.

It is folly to call a relationship based in desire by the name of love. We like to do this because it all sounds so romantic, but love has nothing to do with it. Genuine love is quite another thing. Only an awakened man can love.

## What a Person Really Wants

It is absolutely impossible for you to be disturbed by something you don't want or that disinterests you. This is why we emphasize the need for freedom from false desire. The understanding of desire abolishes what Eastern mystics call *tanha*, that is, painful craving.

Suppose you were given your choice of two peace potions. One of them kept you restful only when events turned out the way you desired. The other one kept you perfectly happy, no matter what happened. Which would you choose? The second one, of course.

Yet, at this very moment, millions of unhappy people in billions of events choose the first. Why do they select the very potion that makes them unhappy? Please listen very carefully. *It is because they have false ideas about what will make them happy.* If we insist that happiness comes from having lots of friends, that is a false and pain-producing idea. If we believe that the easy life will be ours by leaning upon a spouse or upon society, we are in for shock.

To state it another way, we wrongly think happiness occurs when we get what we want. What *does* occur is a thrill, ego-satisfaction or sense of power, none of which is happiness.

Tolstoy points out that when false happiness reaches a certain peak, it turns into grief. This explains the sudden drop into despair of people who finally attain worldly success. What they hoped was a solid mountain turns into a dissolving cloud.

I want to give you a single idea for your constant reflection. Make it your business to grasp its full meaning.

*No man is really interested in getting what he craves. He is really interested in being at peace with himself, but doesn't know how.*

This is why your desires and ambitions change as you learn to think from Supermind. What you used to consider valuable now becomes worthless. What you formerly thought was foolish now is prized.

The most helpful thing you can do for yourself is to be real. To be real is to be everything. The destruction of falseness begins with its detection. Here is one way to start down the road toward being a real person:

Observe your inner states when you are with others. Are you uneasy, timid or do you feel compelled to talk? Next, observe yourself when all alone. Are you more at ease inwardly when by yourself? No doubt you will find this to be so. Here is what to do. Work at being just as relaxed when with others as when all alone. Refuse to permit the mere presence of others to make you nervous. Gradually, but surely, you can banish compulsive behavior when with others; you can remain relaxed.

There is no barrier to your achievement of real selfhood. The supposed barrier is only a mirage of wrong thinking. Take the social situation discussed in the preceding paragraph. There is really no such thing as a tense or uncomfortable situation with others. What really bothers you is the behaviors and explanations you falsely think you owe to others.

You owe nothing to others except to be real, and they owe nothing but the same to you. Do not expect anything else from anyone. They have nothing of true value for you. You alone can give true value to yourself.

## No One Can Possibly Hurt You

Ponder the following dialogue to learn how you can resist all manner of attack upon you.

**Q:** Why do I suffer so much pressure from other people?
**A:** You wrongly give them power over you.

**Q:** If so, I am unaware of it. How do I give them power?
**A:** You do it by falsely attributing power to them. Because you are not as yet reunited with your true self, where genuine power exists, you wrongly assume that power

exists in people, money, excitements and so on. If these things could give you lasting satisfaction in life, how come they haven't?

**Q:** I see what you mean. I've been chasing all my life, but everything is just the same, maybe even worse. But back to the question. How can I be free of hurt from others?

**A:** Inwardly refuse to let the hurtful word or act fall on the negative part of yourself. That makes hurtful feelings impossible. If you refuse to open the door of your house to unwanted strangers, how can they enter? You see, you are unconsciously consenting to being hurt by others. Remind yourself that nothing anyone can say or do can harm the essential you. They can hurt the false self, but you are gradually learning to extinguish your imaginary self and to live only from your original nature.

**Q:** Then it is by living from our true self that we are free from injury?

**A:** Is the beam from a lighthouse affected by howling wind and rain? It remains perfectly steadfast and unaffected by the storm. Your true self is like that. Nothing can ever harm you once you are consciously aware that it is so.

**Q:** I really want to grasp all this.

**A:** Do so, and you will be so different that you won't recognize your former self.

Your social relations change as you learn to think from your Supermind. They change because *you* change. It is a natural process that happens all by itself. Old friends exit and new ones enter. You do not seek people out with the hope of fulfillment from them. You are no longer interested in shallow chatter and artificial activities. More and more you sense that you cannot afford certain relationships. These things happen because of your higher level of psychic success. On this loftier level, you are no longer interested in playing in the basement.

At an advanced point in self-development, you will make the curious discovery that your relations with other people depend entirely on them, not on you. Various people are in or out of your life according to their desires, not yours.

## Seven Guides to Success with People

India's mystical teacher, Sri Ramakrishna, supplies the following illustration:

A large log is immersed in the Ganges River out of sight. A submerged chain connects one end of the log to the riverbank. If you want to reach the log, how will you do it? Well, you cannot see the chain, but you can plunge into the water and follow it. Link by link, you can tug yourself to the log.

One link to self-harmony is daily experience with men and women. The principles of this chapter are not merely aids to social and domestic harmony. Such pleasantness is only a natural expression of a deeper cause, that of self-harmony.

It is too easy to forget that *who we are* determines *what we experience.* So any teaching or system failing to make personal inner transformation its central theme is useless. Only *talk* about peace can come out of it, but never actual peace. And, of course, any individual who fails to make inner change his principle purpose is missing the mark.

With this in mind, we can follow a few links to self-knowledge, leading to human harmony:

1. Whenever disturbed by a memory of a past incident with someone, ask yourself, "But what has that to do with me *right now?*"

2. You can win someone in the right way only when you don't care whether you win him or not.

3. Do not let another's behavior toward you tell you how to behave toward him. Do not respond to gloom with

gloom, nor to rashness with rashness. Behave from you own self.

4. Whatever we subconsciously wish for others, we wish for ourselves. Wishes are psychic boomerangs; we get back what we send out. We must make sure we wish only goodness for both others and ourselves.

5. A person incapable of thinking beyond his own false desires will unconsciously block fulfillment of his true needs.

6. Never look forward to anything. Do not live in excitement of forthcoming social occasions. No, this will not take true pleasure from you. By living fully right now, you live with the only genuine pleasure there is.

7. When living from your Supermind, you less and less find yourself in awkward and unwanted situations. You find yourself more and more where you truly want to be.

## How to Succeed with Difficult People

It helps to realize that hostile people will attack anyone or anything, especially if they detect weakness in another. They shoot their arrows wildly, and if one happens to fall on you, it is merely accidental. You are not a special target. Hostility needs as many targets as possible.

You need not remain a target. Stand up to hostility, not with aggressiveness, but by realizing your own total safety from attempted attack. A hostile person is a weak person who lowers his bow and arrow once he sees you cannot be used for his neurotic needs.

The more you surrender to a difficult person's demands, the more you build his egotism. The more you contribute to his egotism, the more awful you make him. Not only that, but his demands increase. Do you really think a weak person is thankful for charity? We must not be gullible. The ego in man is incapable of gratitude; it angrily demands more.

It is both useless and immoral to serve the demands of weak people, for by doing so, you help destroy them. Several fine points of distinction were brought up in the following conversation.

**Q:** You are right. Why are people so ungrateful? You do something for them and they expect more.

**A:** People are ungrateful for human gifts because they are not what they really want. Human gifts provide a temporary thrill which soon wears off, creating a demand for more shallow thrills. Only cosmic gifts, such as true knowledge, can arouse gratitude.

**Q:** How can I handle unpleasant emotions from others?

**A:** Understand them. If someone is furious, see it as an outburst of his false self. A furious man acts out a false role, having no relation to reality. He has unhealthy notions that life should conform to his demands. Understand the furious man, but never coddle, for that only worsens him.

**Q:** I often feel that my life does not belong to me at all, but to unseen forces.

**A:** Reclaim yourself. Your life does in fact belong to you, not to your acquired habits, society's demands or to a nagging sense of haste.

**Q:** I don't understand. I care for a certain man very much, yet he can be quite cruel at times.

**A:** You may be very fond of your pet dog, but he will still bite you if he is sick.

Behave the way you really are, even if it ends a relationship! Never suppress yourself in an effort to influence, hold or win someone. When we are unreal, so are our rewards. To say this in another way, never behave the way you think the other person wants you to behave, but in the manner you must. Nothing you really need to do or have ever requires a yielding to person or custom.

## The Adventure of True Voyager

A ship named Life set sail for its destination called the Harbor. It carried the usual assortment of passengers found on any ocean voyage.

Running into a battering storm, the ship lost its rudder. The passengers raced around the deck in panic, crying for help. The Officers, who were very proud of being Officers, sought to calm the crowd with assurances that nothing was really wrong. "Just trust us," they repeated, "and all will go well with you."

But there was one True Voyager who wondered about it all. Things were not all right, and he knew it. When he asked the Officers why the rudder was not being repaired, they gave evasive answers. When he insistently asked whether they really knew how to make repairs, they curtly reminded him that their word was not to be questioned.

So True Voyager spent his hours at the rail, searching over the sea for sight of land.

Meanwhile, the Officers had set up Counseling Sessions for the bewildered passengers. Handsomely dressed in their neatly pressed uniforms with bright brass buttons, they smilingly advised, "The rudderless way is the natural way. There is no need to think for yourself; just have faith that you are in good hands. We care for you. As for the Harbor you ask about, it is yours in exchange for obedience to us. When in doubt about anything, just come to us. But don't let your doubts spoil anything. Enjoy yourself, engage in shipboard activities, keep yourself busy."

From time to time, True Voyager tried to persuade the others to join him in his search for land. Hearing of it, the Officers became resentful. In the privacy of their plush quarters, their usual smiles slid away, replaced by dark anger. But the smiles soon reappeared as the Officers stood on deck to warn the passengers about True Voyager: "Beware of that man. He is a strange one. Remain true to your Officers, who care so much for you. We care so much that we don't want to burden you with thinking for yourselves."

Dazzled by the Officers' bright brass buttons, the passengers nodded gratefully, all in unison.

One day while gazing seaward, True Voyager sighted land. He called to the others who were seated on deck in a Counseling Session. They sat stiffly, as if in a hypnotic trance, their faces dazedly reflecting the dazzle of the Officers' bright brass buttons.

Knowing they could not hear him, True Voyager turned away. Leaping overboard, he swam to solid ground.

## For Pleasant Human Relations

1. Your Supermind knows how to act in every situation for your benefit.

2. Uplift your level of cosmic awareness and harmony follows.

3. See that people are not at all what they seem to be.

4. Understand yourself and you will understand others.

5. Use contacts with your fellow man as a means of psychic growth.

6. In the Supermind-life, you are not dominated by any one or any group.

7. Think with your unfailing Supermind, not with human reasoning, for fulfilled living.

8. To be real in Cosmic Truth is to be everything anyone could desire.

9. No person and no event has any power to harm you.

# 9

# How to Clear Up Problems Quickly with Supermind

If your usual attempts to clear your day of problems have not succeeded, you need not be discouraged. You were not born to lose. You need only realize that the way out lies in an entirely new direction. This refreshing way is rarely tried by most people, which is why most people remain troubled.

The answers to life exist. There is no question about that. The only question is, do we want them in preference to what we now accept as answers?

We must examine again a foremost principle of *Supermind: Man dwells in a peculiar kind of psychic sleep of which he has not the slightest suspicion. But he can and must wake up. Then, he knows the answers.*

Count Leo Tolstoy describes his own life while under psychic hypnosis like this:

He was in a boat in the middle of a stream. He could see a distant shore, but because it was unknown to him, he hesitated. Not knowing what to do with himself, he glanced around at other boats in the stream. They were drifting downstream. Assuming that they knew what they were doing, he relaxed his oars and drifted dreamily downstream with them. But to his sudden horror, he sighted destructive rapids ahead, breaking up the other boats. Shocked into independent action, he tugged hard at the oars, bringing himself back to the safe shore originally sighted.

The shore was his spiritual destiny, his cosmic homeland. The oars were his power of right action, which he had previously abandoned to the careless thinking of drifting men, but which he recovered for his own rescue.

When we wake up, all else is added, including answers to perplexities. If we try to add all else before awakening, we add nothing of lasting value. That would be like one of the drifting men finding a gold coin in his boat — just before plunging into the rapids.

## We Must Learn to Think Clearly

There is no human difficulty that cannot be solved by clear thinking. Yes, you need nothing more than to go your way with a clear mind in order to make it a good way.

Now, this may seem too simple an approach. We are so in the habit of looking for complicated theories or scholarly conclusions. They are unnecessary. All we need to do is clear our minds of mental weeds, making fruitful growth possible. In this book, we are discussing profound cosmic principles. We are exploring the ideas of men like Krishnamurti and Gurdjieff, and examining systems like Zen and Sufism. Also, a special term has been created, that of the Supermind.

We have done all this for the single purpose of clarifying the mind, so that the life may be changed.

Now, the trouble is, people think that they already think clearly. No matter how often they meet tragedy and misery, people simply will not believe that there is something wrong with their mental processes. They never learn the lesson taught by conflict. Instead, they chase to a new doctrine, a popular amusement or a familiar face, hoping for the relief which never comes. It is like a man lost in the desert whose panic leads him even farther astray.

If you suffer financial loss, your solution is to think clearly toward it, and nothing else. Whether you accept this or not, I assure you it is a fact. If you suffer from aching loneliness, there is a harbor of thinking which loneliness cannot enter. You can know this state for yourself. If you are afraid of what will become of you, the clear thinking of the Supermind can banish that fear. If you do not know what to do with your life, you can learn to think with an amazing simplicity where confusion is impossible.

We can look at Augustine as an example of how the mind can change the man. Augustine was taunted by lesser men who reminded him of his youthful follies. He took it calmly, without negative reaction, knowing that his very nature had changed and that folly was no longer part of him. He may have taken part in the following exchange of questions and answers:

**Q:** You once said that the Supermind can correct past mistakes. How is it possible to change history?

**A:** Self-history is what the mind makes it. You can change your mind and so change your concept of yourself. Don't give the mere memory of a past mistake power over you. It has none. You can remember the actual incident, but don't think it has anything to do with you *today*. You are a new person every single moment.

**Q:** My life is one frustration after another. I am always doing things in the hope they will do me some good, but I end up right back where I started. The greater the hope, the harder the flop. Why?

**A:** You falsely assume that you know what is good for you. You do not presently know how to serve yourself lasting goodness. Acting from false beliefs is as vain as setting a fish net out in the desert. Learn the ways of your own mind.

**Q:** But why can't I make progress by following my adopted beliefs?

**A:** Because if the road is wrong, you will go wrong. You can't reach New York by taking the road to Chicago.

## You Have Abundant Riches in Cosmic Self

No matter how stormy your affairs, nothing compels you to remain where you are. The storm that has cut off your communication with your true self need not be permanent. The free life arising from the clarity of the Supermind can be lived any time, any place, by anyone.

There are ways to break through the psychic walls of misunderstanding. If you can break through a wall of paper, you can break through a wall of brick, but you must start with paper.

Where can we start to think in favor of ourselves? Fortunately, we can start anywhere, just as the determined swimmer dives into the sea at any point. You can begin to suspect that what you want may not be the same thing as what is best for the essential you. This is not as easy as it seems, for nagging desires are very clever at masquerading as authentic needs.

We can see that merely thinking about happiness and actually living happily are two different things. It is the difference between imagining a colorful meadow and actually standing in that meadow. If we carelessly take the imaginative picture as the living reality, we unconsciously cheat ourselves. The mass of men and women do this very thing. The way out is to suspect that the mental picture is nothing more than a picture. Sometimes sharp shock or severe suffering awakens within us the hint of something real beyond the mere thought.

Make this simple test of your efforts: Ask, "Do I truly see things a bit more clearly than before?" If so, it is genuine gain. If not, you need only patiently persist in clearing away the mental fog.

Consistently place yourself closer and closer to the secret source within yourself. The source itself becomes your newness. It is like a grove of trees bordering a river. The greenness and vitality of each individual tree is determined by its closeness to the river.

You cannot do, achieve or have anything without that stately power we call self-responsibility. You cannot abandon yourself and expect to enrich yourself. All poverty is self-poverty, all riches are self-riches.

You have no power that is not a gift from yourself, no happiness except that which springs from the true you, no freedom other than the freedom of your own natural state.

Whatever you give yourself can never be taken from you. It endures forever. Any thought that is your thought, any honor that is your honor, is not subject to change or destruction. It is an eternal possession.

But whatever is given you by other individuals or by organizations can and will be taken away. Honors and rewards conferred on men by men are only stage performances, with the curtain ready to drop.

Shun the gifts that men give to men. They are empty and we sense it. Learn to give to yourself. You will find that these self-gifts alone are honorable, real and immortal.

## How The Supermind Solves Problems

Here is how I explained humanly conditioned workings of the mind to one of my questioners:

**Q:** You speak often about the terrible conflicts in people. While there are troubles in life, most people seem fairly calm.

**A:** It is vital that you understand. It is utter illusion that people are calm. Two things produce the illusion. First, everyone is an expert actor in concealing deep conflicts behind false fronts. Secondly, as long as a crisis is absent, anyone can go around appearing in control. But let the smallest emergency come along and he falls apart. You have no idea of the hidden horror of those who appear self-controlled.

**Q:** Isn't this a pessimistic view?

**A:** Is a doctor pessimistic when he sees illness as illness? Wouldn't he be an incompetent doctor if he saw a sick man as healthy? And wouldn't his so-called optimism be the very barrier to successful treatment?

**Q:** Yes, of course.

**A:** Contrived optimism is pessimism.

We must realize the incapacity of the conditioned mind to solve problems. It is the *cause* of problems. It cannot cure itself. By the conditioned mind we mean the mind made up of borrowed ideas, personal ambitions, deceptive reasonings. Such a fixed mind cannot discover what is best; it can only seek frantically for what it thinks it must have.

Let's see how a man burdened with fixed attitudes tries to solve a problem. Let's say he feels betrayed or offended by someone. His first mistake is to let the event tell him how to feel. It commands him to be angry, nervous, upset. He falls for the command, which sets the scene for the next tragic act of thinking of ways to restore his hurt feelings. He tells everyone how badly he was treated. He inwardly complains and feels sorry for himself. If revenge is possible, he takes it, while justifying himself. If there is no way to strike back, he runs mental movies of revenge through his mind.

What a terrible tragedy. Do you think that man will listen if you try to explain what he is doing to himself? No, he takes a peculiar enjoyment from his negativities, not knowing the price he pays.

Now we can take the same event of betrayal and see how a man thinking from his Supermind handles it. Firstly, he would not let the event dictate the nature of his feelings. He is not a puppet jerked this way and that by exterior events; he is self-directed. Next, *betrayal does not even exist for him.* Only the egotistical self feels betrayed; only the false center feels a sense of injustice. The man is truly untouchable. Having no false center, he cannot react falsely, that is, with anger or distress.

Do not think this Supermind-man is weak or indifferent because he does not flare up at seeming betrayals. He is so strong, so very strong, that he shrugs his shoulders at seeming attacks upon him. It is the weak man who feels betrayed.

All this calls for us to transform our thinking toward ourselves and our daily events. We don't want to react the way most people do. They are miserable, and you don't want to be like most people. You want to be changed, different.

## The Solution to Nervousness

If you run your hand down a knotted rope, it disturbs the hand. If you want it smooth, you must untie the knots. The knots in life are all the wrong ideas picked up from other people with knotted ropes.

There is a familiar anecdote about the young bride whose biscuits turned out hard and untasty. When her husband gently hinted of it, she objected, "But they couldn't be tasteless — the cookbook says they're delicious!"

Beneath the humor is found an error common to unhappy people. Whenever their wrong ideas are questioned, they come up with irrelevant replies. It goes something like this:

**Q:** Are you happy?
**A:** My religion says I am.
**Q:** But are you happy?
**A:** I follow traditional beliefs.
**Q:** But are you happy?
**A:** My friends think I am.
**Q:** But are you happy?
**A:** I have faith and hope.
**Q:** But are you happy?
**A:** Well, I don't exactly know what to say now.

To merely chatter about solutions is no good, regardless of how intelligent the words may seem. Fast replies and popular opinions lead nowhere. Erasmus calls this shallowness *verbal shrewdness.*

There is one right path and a thousand wrong ones. Let's examine one of the misleading ways.

A troubled mind immediately goes to work to manufacture answers, useless ones. Answers manufactured by the imitative mind are no answers at all; they are useless chasings.

Suppose a man feels bored and restless. His mind anxiously searches around for relief. It comes up with several possibilities. He can go to the sports arena. There is a lively cafe down the street. He can plunge into a new business project. He can try to meet a woman.

Nothing can come of it. None will do more than suspend his nervousness for a short time, because he mistakes an *escape* for an *answer.* He falsely assumes that the solution is somewhere outside himself. He fails to see that the answer is within the very problem. It is the same as if he tried to run away from his own body!

*There was a man who was frightened at his shadow ....* *He did not know that if he stayed in a shady place, his shadow would have disappeared.* (Chuang-tse)

The strange part of it is man's inability to see false answers *as* false answers. No matter how often he wakes up with the same headache, the familiar nerves, the habitual anger, he stumbles right back to the same blunders.

Then there is the Supermind solution. It is a shady place. It comes when the mind grows weary, gives up, dares to know nothing and abandons itself to something unknown and indescribable.

## The Power of Self-Awakening of Supermind

Fire departments wisely spend much of their time in fire prevention, giving them fewer fires to fight. So does the wise individual discover ways to prevent problems from flaming up in the first place.

The Supermind-way makes it unnecessary to fight one problem after another. You are above all problems. This is not an ideal in which to believe. It is a fact to make your own.

*A desperation to escape a problem is the wrong way. A passion to understand it is the right way.*

When finding yourself in an awkward situation in the Outer World, you need not struggle. Just go along with it as a detached observer. Do not become upset at whatever happens, but stand apart within your Inner World in silent understanding. This draws all the hurt from the situation. If your grand purpose in life is to wake up, then whatever happens to you is good, for it can prod you into self-awakening. But if you have wrong aims which serve false purposes, whatever happens will be self-defeating.

Most people find it difficult to see that it is their attitude that makes an event seem either good or bad. One corrective technique is to take some small annoyance and try to see it with a different viewpoint. Work sincerely to see the event or the person in a new way. Remember, this new and liberating way exists as a fact whether you are aware of it or not. Your task is personal discovery of it.

The questioning of presently-held viewpoints is an absolute necessity for self-transformation. It means that you must go against your old and familiar ways of thinking. It means you must think, act and feel the exact opposite of other people. As Christian remarked in *Pilgrim's Progress, If you will go with us, you must go against wind and tide ....*

The seeing and taking of life in a fresh manner is the very heart of the Supermind-way. Incidentally, what has your present way given you? Possibly you see yourself asking the following questions:

**Q:** I know how practical you are with your esoteric ideas, so I'd like to ask about my problem of insomnia. How can I get to sleep without pills?

**A:** Stop fighting sleeplessness. Your very fear of not sleeping is what keeps you awake. If your mind and body do not want to sleep, why should you object? Give up caring whether you sleep or not.

**Q:** You once said there is nothing I need do about my problems, and also that I can do everything about them. Please explain.

**A:** The conditioned self made up of contradictory desires and false viewpoints can do nothing but fall even deeper into the pit. But the new you, the Supermind-self, your cosmic consciousness, knows the answer to everything. This new you can reach the point where it needs no answers because it has no questions.

## How Problems Can Disappear Into Their Native Nothingness

Problems disappear when your thoughts, words and acts agree with your inner essence, that is, with your true self. Disharmony consists of contradiction between what is true and what is falsely assumed to be true.

Take the problem of overweight. It arises because the wrong center takes charge of a person. Overweight cannot occur when we let the body, not the mind, tell us when to eat. Do you see the importance of self-acquaintance?

Take problems connected with money. The self-unified man has an entirely different relation to money than the self-divided man. For one thing, he is far more practical. He spends for what he really needs, not for artificial needs aroused by possessiveness. Having no compulsive need for the sense of power provided by the spending of money, he spends less and needs less. He cannot be attracted, tempted or bribed by wealth. That is one of his peaceful liberties.

We can learn something by recalling the classic tale of the Gordian Knot. Hundreds of years ago there existed the tiny Asian kingdom of Phrygia. Its sole claim to fame rested on a special wagon in one of the courtyards. The wagon was fastened to a yoke by an astonishing knot called the Gordian Knot. It was prophesied that whoever untied the knot would conquer the world. But for more than 100 years, the Gordian Knot defied all efforts of clever kings and warriors.

Alexander, the young King of Macedonia, journeyed to Phrygia to try his hand. Upon the appointed day, the courtyard swarmed with curious spectators. All others had failed, they reasoned, so what new method could succeed for Alexander?

Drawing his sword, Alexander cleanly sliced the knot in two.

I tell this story to emphasize a point made at the start of this chapter. We must learn an entirely new method of severing our difficulties. The best part of it is that a new method exists. It is something entirely different from what you may imagine it is. If the answer can be imagined, it is not authentic. The solution to every human problem is not a matter of imagination, but a matter of fact. Only facts can give us greatness. *All men can do great things, if they know what great things are.* (Samuel Butler)

People blithely assume they have a choice between being happy with the spiritual life or happy without it. There is no such choice. We are either happy with the truth or unhappy without it. There is no compromise.

Sooner or later, you must rise up and refuse to be victimized any longer by the tyrannies within yourself. You might as well do it now. Make the motto of your life: *No compromise with mental integrity.*

## How Supermind Transformed a War Lord

Peace on earth? What about worldwide problems which affect every individual?

Individual inner transformation is the only way to social peace. That means you and me. But since the majority of men refuse to see social sickness as a projection of their own maladjustments, the problem persists. Man prefers to evade his personal responsibility by pretending that the cause is somewhere outside himself. He does not change for the good; he merely rearranges the bad. That is like transferring a hospital patient from one bed to another in the hope it will cure him. *Finally, the mind of man is so fashioned that it is subject much more to disguises than with realities.* (Erasmus)

Emperor Asoka of ancient India provides a perfect example of social peace through individual inner transformation. Trained in warfare as a young prince, Asoka later conquered neighboring lands, with all the usual casualties and griefs. Coming under the influence of esoteric teachings, including those of Buddha, Asoka changed into an entirely new man. Renouncing war and cruelty, he became a model monarch by his example of strength through spiritual insight. Let me answer the questions I anticipate you would ask as follows:

**Q:** You say that we must clearly see the madness of the world. But won't this be frightening?

**A:** That is an enormously important question. No, it is frightening only when you *don't* see, when you fail to grasp the true cause. When clearly seen, fright is impossible. The free man sees social madness unemotionally, impersonally, like he would observe caged tigers clawing at each other.

**Q:** What is the Supermind solution to the social problem of crime, for example, theft?

**A:** All crimes are caused by psychic hypnosis. A group of men are walking in the countryside. One of them thinks he sees a cobra. In his fright he steals another man's stick to fight it. But in his clarified vision he realizes that it was not a cobra after all, only a rope. He no longer steals because he doesn't need the stick. False seeing produces false need, which produces false behavior.

**Q:** I would like to study all this, but there are so many conflicting teachers and systems. To which one should I listen?

**A:** If you are surrounded by a dozen people, all speaking at once, attention is impossible. Cut them off. Listen to yourself only. One of the speakers may tell you the truth, but you can neither recognize nor value his wisdom until you have at least a bit of it in yourself. It is useless to depend upon another. Once you recognize true wisdom when you hear it, you can safely listen to a true teacher for further guidance.

## How to Give True Meaning to Life

You anxiously and endlessly plan to take either this or that course of action. You want to make sure you don't make a mistake. After painfully switching back and forth between this and that, you finally decide to do this. If it turns out pleasurably, you congratulate yourself on your wise decision; if you get hurt, you dislike yourself. What you don't realize is that there is no difference between this and that. There is only a difference in the way you reacted. You reacted with pleasure toward the first outcome because it gave you a protective sense of being right, of not being wrong. You felt safe for the moment, but worried about the next action.

It is this desperate need to be right that must be tossed aside. It is achieved by doing whatever you do without caring whether you are right or wrong, by being indifferent to results. When living from the Supermind, you don't care whether you are right or wrong and thus have no anxiety.

It is total involvement with life, without preconceived notions of what is best for us, that turns the tide. In that involvement there is neither ego-excitement nor ego-hurt, only reality, which is supremacy.

*But if men who do not see life would only approach nearer to the phantoms which alarm them, and would examine them, they would perceive that for them also they are only phantoms, and not realities.* (Leo Tolstoy)

No condition in the Outer World can bother you when living from your Inner World. There are no unanswered questions, whether concerned with voting for a candidate, your career, whether to marry or not, alcohol, tipping the waiter, dressing correctly, whether dealing with policemen or calories or unbalanced people.

Heraclitus, the ancient mystic, provides an example for any modern man who wishes to live in the world but wants no part of its confusion. Born of noble rank, Heraclitus found himself deeply involved in the social and political wranglings of his native Ephesus. He saw all the professed ideals of ambitious men as clever masks for their selfish strivings. Unable to compromise his inner integrity, he abandoned the city to find quietude in the countryside. From there he sent his inspiring messages back to those who also wanted something better. Heraclitus declared that both personal peace and social stability is achieved only when mankind lives and thinks from cosmic intelligence. An earnest seeker for cosmic intelligence once probed for my answers as follows:

**Q:** But the noise of modern living is so distracting.

**A:** There need be no conflict between today's living and inner awakening. Electronic computers and television sets are not enemies in themselves. They hamper us only when we make them false gods. A self-discovered businessman can stand before a clicking computer and be perfectly at ease.

**Q:** What is the meaning of life? One day I feel I have found it, but the next day am downcast again. *Is* there meaning to life?

**A:** Please understand. This question is asked out of anxiety, which prevents your understanding. But let's see. As long as you desire life to have a meaning based on conditioned ideas, meaning eludes you. All attempts based on untrue ideas must produce false meanings, which fall apart. You can answer your own question with earnest exploration. Willingly drop all frantic efforts to give meaning to life. Let the emptiness which is there *be* there, and you will understand.

# How to Be a Psychic Detective

People do not really solve their problems. They merely exchange one trial for another. Everything remains the same; they only pretend anything is different. The glimpse that this is so can start the ending of this kind of dreariness.

A man attracts the kind of problems he has because of the kind of person he is. His negative nature duplicates itself outwardly, wherever he goes. A quarrelsome person inevitably finds himself quarreling with others. A person feeling that others will take advantage of him will actually find himself being taken. Those who reject the psychic facts of life have no choice but to encounter one rejection after another.

You *do* what you *are*. To change what you do, change who you are.

There is no use trying to do anything with exterior conditions of a negative nature. They are mere shadows, cast by the wolf-nature within a man. It is futile to fight or cover up a shadow. The wolf itself must be destroyed. That is the task of the Supermind.

The places you visit indicate your psychic level. You are where you are because of who you are. Your attendance at a dinner, lecture, picnic, business conference, etc., connects with your level of consciousness. As you rise in self-awareness, your visits change their character and become healthier. This is a good example of how a man's life in his Inner World determines his activities in the Outer World. As Chuang-tse remarks, *Given this truth within, it exercises a spiritual efficacy without, and this is why we count it so valuable.*

With all this in mind, how can an earnest seeker go to work for himself? He can be a psychic detective by noticing the connection between the way he thinks and what happens to him. He can see the origin of problems as within himself. He can know the impossibility of obtaining newness through changing outer conditions. He can get new television programs by changing his television set. He can understand the existence of repetitive forces within him that repeat negative circumstances.

When a man actually sees the dreadful price he pays for his unconscious negativities, he stops them. No man *consciously* harms himself. If he does not stop, he does not see. We always feel bad whenever we do something against our true interests. This can be a great clue for self-correction. Problems and pains always accompany a self-harming thought or action. There is something within trying to awaken us. We can cooperate by trying to open our eyes.

There is no use trying to build a clock with a gardener's tools. But there are right tools for creating a clock. Likewise, you can start today to use the right tools of your Supermind to create the spacious life.

## Basic Principles of Chapter 9

1. The way out of confusion lies in an entirely new direction with Supermind.

2. The answer to every problem lies in a clear mind based in Cosmic Truth.

3. Come closer to the secret source of cosmic wisdom within you.

4. Take total self-responsibility for your psychic growth.

5. Whatever you give to yourself with Supermind cannot be taken away from you.

6. The Supermind cures ills caused by faulty thought.

7. Have no fear of inner emptiness of your soul with Supermind.

8. Inner negativity reproduces itself outwardly.

9. To change what you do, change who you are.

# 10

## Facts of Cosmic Life for True Happiness in Supermind

A good but unhappy king stood in his courtyard, gazing anxiously over the castle walls toward the sea. A wise man had told the king that a great ship was on its way, carrying a rare manuscript revealing the secrets of Happiness.

Finally, the ship was sighted. In his desperation to get the manuscript, the king sent out his navy to urge the approaching ship to greater speed. But frightened at the sight of the armed fleet, the ship turned and sailed away.

A few days later, the ship was again sighted as it made its way toward anchor in the king's harbor. But once more the impatient monarch blundered. In his haste to direct its course, his signals went wrong. The incoming ship was caught in an adverse current, and was swept back out to sea.

Tired of being thwarted by his own misdirected efforts, the king resolved to let the ship arrive in its own way. With that, the ship reached harbor, giving the monarch the secrets of Happiness.

Readers who have studied Eastern wisdom, such as Zen, will see the lesson here. It is simply stated: *By ceasing to interfere with your own happiness, it arrives.*

How do we unknowingly interfere? Well, for one thing, by doubting the possibility of newness.

Happiness is quite possible. No doubt about it. The only doubt is whether we will abandon our frozen notions about the nature of happiness. *All men wish to be happy, but are dull at perceiving exactly what it is that makes life happy.* (Seneca)

# The Exploration of Happiness

To grasp the real meaning of happiness, we must think toward it with utmost clarity. Start by seeing that happiness is not the presence of an exciting feeling, but the absence of a painful feeling. When you feel no mental pain — conscious or unconscious — you are happy. In other words, true happiness is not the opposite of pain, but the absence of pain.

In other sections we saw that heartache can be abolished and contentment established. But, we also saw that people do not want to give up painful feelings because they provide emotional stimulation. This is counterfeit contentment. Unhappy people wonder how they can possibly survive without their great storehouse of negativity. That is like wondering how to get along without a sinking ship.

It is really quite fantastic. Man fears the very quietness he seeks!

Already we have some clearness of mind. We see our goal as the elimination of pain, not the pursuit of excitement.

All this answers a question which I am frequently asked, "Shouldn't we concentrate on positive items, like peace and love, rather than explore negativities, like heartache and human badness?"

No, there is no use discussing peace as long as the problem is pain. If you stub your toe, do you treat your hand? Peace is the absence of pain, so that is where we must concentrate our attention. This is why esoteric writings, like the

Upanishads, point out that the solution to a problem is found in the problem itself, not away from it.

You see, we want to know the truth about things. And the truth is the warmest, friendliest, most positive and loving force in the universe.

It is quite easy to see the cause of unhappiness. We cannot reject the facts of life and have their happiness, any more than we can refuse a coat on a cold day and feel warm. We miss the most obvious things; for instance, we fail to see that our *ideas about happiness* are not the same thing as *happiness itself.*

## Mere Excitement is Not Happiness

Understanding our sorrow is pure magic. When sorrow is truly understood, it ceases to be sorrow.

What must we understand? We can realize that physical and emotional thrills contribute absolutely nothing to the essential self or to inner harmony. As long as we mistakenly identify with them and think they are a part of the secret self, we are caught up in endless craving and frustration. It is difficult at first for the mind to see that fleeting pleasure is not the same thing as abiding contentment. It cannot conceive the idea that above a mere idea about happiness, there is another Happiness.

Also, happiness is impossible if we think it will come when we achieve this or that future objective. Only the present moment is alive, therefore, only in the here and now can happiness be in motion. We would not try to enjoy a musical composition when it is finished; we appreciate it from note to note.

Here is what to do: Behave as if you have no ideas at all as to what will make you happy. Know nothing whatsoever about what can bring it about.

Do you see what this does? It destroys our illusions that we already know. We don't know, otherwise, we would be happy. But, no one notices this contradiction. See how one person grasped the significance by his asking the following questions.

**Q:** That is such a different idea. Could we discuss it?

**A:** Reflect upon this strange secret of happiness: If you do not know what will make you happy, do you have a problem? No. Only when you assume that you know are you in conflict, for then you must decide between several possible courses. You must decide whether to marry or not, whether to move to another city and so on. But suppose your mind was blank, having no possibilities. In that blankness is quietness.

**Q:** Then it is the civil war between various false ideas that cause the grief. Yes, I see it. Still, we have to *think*.

**A:** You have to think *clearly*, not from muddled notions. This is quite possible, I assure you.

**Q:** What a very strange secret!

**A:** Do not be afraid of having a blank mind. And do not think it represents indecision. It is the very key that unlocks the door to higher consciousness.

## Two Vital Steps to Contentment

What do you consider to be a major cause of unhappiness? Some will charge it to lack of financial success. Others will say it is an unsatisfactory marriage. More will say it is failure to attain a particular goal.

Most people could attribute their sadness to the frustration of their various desires. So let's probe the Supermind solution.

Here is the great secret for satisfying every desire you have: Desire only what is truly necessary. But *there* is where we must throw every ounce of insight into the battle. We must distinguish between true and false needs. Otherwise, we condemn ourselves to the butterfly life, forever flittering and never resting.

At this moment, millions of people on earth are getting exactly what they subconsciously request — to their sorrow. It is necessary to see the connection between our state of happiness and our supposed needs. For instance, the desperate need to escape a problem is the wrong way. A passion for understanding it is the right way.

*Self-awareness* brings daily relief by showing us the difference between what we think we need and what we really need. False needs spring from human vanity, true needs from the cosmic self.

A Sufi story tells of a teacher and his student who were traveling together. The pupil carried several pieces of gold which he thought his teacher knew nothing about.

They came to a dark valley where the road split into two choices. Fearful that robbers might steal his gold, the student asked, "Which road should we take?" His teacher replied, "Get rid of the possessions which make you afraid and either road is good."

The possessions which make us afraid consist of our false concepts about ourselves. Nothing else ever has or ever will make a human being afraid. To overcome this, ask yourself how you would feel if you *did* lose your present concepts. At first you would feel empty, and then you would both feel and be fulfilled. You are not your changeable feelings; you are something which cannot be changed by anything.

In summary, do these two things:

1. *Let go of the false.*

2. *Endure to the end the temporary increase in anxiety created by the vacuum.*

That is all there is to it. That is all you need to do and can do. The miracle then happens of itself. The True, having been made welcome by your conscious acceptance of the vacuum, comes to you with quiet power.

## Why Things Happen As They Do

People feel unjustly punished by daily events: the boss criticizes their work, expenses exceed income, expected benefits fail to come. People react as if these are some sort of punishments which they don't deserve.

There are two major points to understand about punishment:

1. When you learn to think from your Supermind what you formerly thought was punishment ceases to be so. Although the same events can transpire, they are no longer seen as acts against you. They are merely impersonal incidents. Seen as neutral incidents, they cannot cause pain.

2. All punishment is self-punishment. We may not realize it, but we are never punished by the event, but by our faulty response to it. If we correct the reaction, we abolish both self-punishment and our unconscious fears.

Men and women are filled with unconscious fears. A man's automobile breaks down and the nervous reflex "How much will this cost me?" spoils his day. A woman wants a man's assurance that he loves her, but fears he may be incapable of it no matter how much she sacrifices to him.

You must refuse to live like this and your refusal is the first step.

One of the despairs of men and women is the false belief in their inability to do something for themselves. The aim of *Supermind* is to prove that something can be done — something more magnificent than can be imagined. *Without effort, he rules all things by the power of his mind.* (Xenophanes)

Try to see that a thought about a person or event is merely a *thought about* that person or event. It is the thought about them that makes you feel the way you do. To change the way you feel, change the way you think. This can be done by anyone. I have no doubt for you. I know what you can do as I told another person in answer to his questions in the following exchange:

**Q:** Why do things happen as they do? Does chance govern everything that happens to us?

**A:** There is no such thing as chance. Everything happens as it must happen. It appears to be chance because we did not expect certain things to happen. We expect events to turn out according to our desires or fears, and then are surprised when they turn out differently.

**Q:** Can you give an example?

**A:** You hope to drive to the beach in a half hour, but find it takes an hour. All sorts of causes came together and crossed over to make it an hour. They included the weather, a detour, your state of mind which determined your driving speed and so on. A thousand definite but unseen factors added up to make the result what it was. Mere chance had no place in it.

**Q:** What about inner events, like happiness and misery?

**A:** They are also determined by definite factors, like attitudes, emotions, flexibility, mental maturity. Once the inner causes are right, your reactions to outer events are right. Arriving at the beach a half hour later than desired cannot make you unhappy; being unhappy is what makes you unhappy. Try to see unexpected events as merely *different*, not as *unpleasant*.

## The Superior Way to Serenity with Supermind

How many people do you know who are really happy? I don't mean active, successful or smiling; I mean truly happy. How many behave with the same pleasant calmness in private that they act out in public?

A good place to notice this wide gap is in our family and close friends. But the perfect place to notice it is in ourselves! This is self-science at its best.

164

A ruthless honesty about our present state of happiness is essential if we are to change things. *It is very necessary that a man should be appraised early in life that it is a masquerade in which he finds himself. For otherwise there are many things which he will fail to understand ....* (Arthur Schopenhauer)

There is false happiness and there is true happiness. Our interesting task is to distinguish between the two. We must learn to recognize whatever is harmful to us, for in that instant of recognition, it forever loses its power to harm.

Because he lives in a state of psychic sleep, a man thinks the question is, "Well, do I want my happiness in the form of money, power or fame?" In reality, the question is, "Do I want genuine happiness or do I want the pretense of it?"

Have you ever noticed the many ideas you have as to what can make you happy? Everyone has dozens of such ideas, including the gaining of more money, the winning of new romance and love, a change in social life.

Now, the *Supermind* approach is entirely different. It has nothing to do with changing externals. External events are, after all, merely the result of inner causes. So the *Supermind* has an approach all its own, which is:

*We change our ideas about what it means to be happy.*

That is the sure method by which true happiness is attained. It can be used by anyone for success.

## Your Inner Self Is Free from Contaminated Impressions

Whoever is contented with himself is superior to a wealthy king, for the king cannot give him anything. The contented man is free of the snare of gifts.

True happiness is independent of everything. It knows nothing whatsoever of financial loss, poor health or advancing years. Like a towering mountain, it cannot be shaken by earthly winds. Meister Eckhart describes this strength as follows: *The exterior man may be undergoing trials, although the interior man is quite free ....*

How much happiness have you when things do not happen as you wish? If you do not get upset, you are doing fine. But be careful. Do not think that suppression of unhappiness means peace. No! Covering the kettle does not cool the boiling soup. Happiness is not the suppression of upset feelings, but their absence.

Do not deny yourself the normally nice pleasantries of the world in the belief that they are anti-spiritual. People who do this merely repress themselves, which results in secret bitterness and neurosis. Participate freely in your business and social activities, but do not form attachments to them in an effort to find security.

Also, never try to be more spiritually advanced than you are. That is a painful trap. Be exactly who you are at this present moment. When you do this, change occurs. However, *you* don't change anything, it just changes.

Buddha found this secret to true happiness. In the early years of his search he practiced severe self-denial, including fasting. On one occasion he so weakened himself that his friends could hardly pull him out of a raging river. Seeing the folly of exterior exercise, he turned in the right direction — inner insight.

Do not run mental movies through your mind in the way you want a future event to happen. It will happen the way it must happen, regardless of your imagined wish. If you simply let it happen, whether or not it coincides with your desires, you will not be disappointed. But if you insist that the outcome must match your mental movie, frustration is certain.

Whatever happens is the right thing to happen. Does this challenge your present ideas? Well, good. Drop all mental movies. Leave the screen blank. Reality can then project its own love scene.

## How to Change Your Ways of Conditioned Thinking

The dissatisfaction of most people is not a sharp stab, but a dull ache. It doesn't bite; it gnaws. One kind of lingering discontent shared by millions is the notion that others are happier than they are. I assure you, they are not. If you could only see the secret sorrows of those whose smiles and activities seem to indicate happiness. If you could only see how fervently they wish to be somewhere else, doing something different, being someone other than who they are.

A genuinely happy man is one in a million because an authentically free man is one in a million. You can, if you wish, be that one in a million. However, you must work and be sincere. You must abandon the notion that you already know the answers. You must try. If you will fill the requirements, nothing will be impossible to you.

Know that unnatural thinking is the cause of all unnatural conditions. Also know the other side of the gold coin — natural thinking is the cause of natural satisfaction. It was difficult to convince my questioner as follows, but undoubtedly he became enlightened.

**Q:** I don't understand how changing my mind can change my inner condition. For example, how can a new way of thinking make me happier?

**A:** Let's take one type of thinking — desire. If an outcome harmonizes with your desire, you call it good and feel elated. But if the outcome is contrary to what you want, you call it bad and feel sad. You mistakenly think the outcome itself possesses good or bad, which it does not. Do you see that the reaction is within the person, not within the outcome?

**Q:** Yes, that's right.

**A:** Do you also see that it is merely a conditioned opinion on your part that the event is either good or bad? For instance, one man is excited over money-making activities while another is bored.

**Q:** Logical, but it still is not as clear as it should be to me.

**A:** Now, why do you desire an event to turn out in a certain way? It is because you assume it will add something to your inner self, perhaps security or pleasure. It can give you neither, though it can supply illusions of security and pleasure. Now we come to the heart of things. Suppose you change your thinking so that you no longer automatically label results as either good or bad. Suppose you simply see them as events which can neither add true happiness nor subtract it. In that new way of thinking, you could never be hurt by an event, nor could it provide false elation that later swings over to depression.

**Q:** But if an event happens to me, I must react in some way.

**A:** Yes, but it will not be the false reaction of the invented self. The new you will react correctly. All this becomes clear as soon as you drop your false sense of identity. By seeing that you are not the kind of person you assumed you were, you lose the difficulties you assumed that you had.

**Q:** I don't want to put up with one particular difficulty any longer. Do I have to?

**A:** You do not have to put up with it, whatever it is. Not as long as you realize the one essential fact that the problem is always within you, never outside. By working correctly with yourself, the difficulty vanishes.

## How Loss Can Be Your Gain

If it takes apparent misfortune to turn us into true philosophers and doers of good to receive good, then apparent misfortune is our greatest fortune. A remarkable man named Boethius proved this by personal experience.

Born into a distinguished Roman family about 480, Boethius pursued the double career of statesman and philosopher. His insight into both spiritual and human affairs carried him to this conclusion: *Only those who first obey cosmic laws are qualified to administer human laws. But how few there are!*

As is usual with men of authentic integrity, Boethius aroused the hostility of entrenched authorities. At the height of his success and fortune, he was falsely accused by the very people he tried to advise. Sentenced to prison, Boethius turned his mind toward the deeper meaning of life on earth. Out of his reflections came a simple but powerful book, *The Consolation of Philosophy*. Very popular in Europe for several hundred years, it is still appreciated around the world.

We can summarize some of the more important findings of Boethius as follows:

1. The perfect and abiding source of happiness is possession of the true self.

2. *Genuine love truly binds men and women together; artificial love only appears to do so.*

3. Misfortune in earthly affairs can be surmounted in every case, and replaced with true wisdom and tranquility.

4. *While riches and good fortune are not bad in themselves, they must not divert one from the true riches of the Inner World.*

5. We must understand and break the power of false desires.

6. *The help a seeker needs is always available, if only he seeks it sincerely.*

7. The genuinely spiritual life and genuine happiness are one and the same.

8. *The mind, like a field, must be cleared of weeds, so that natural wealth may grow abundantly.*

9. When personal troubles are used properly, they lead to higher realms of understanding.

10. *We must realize that absolutely nothing has real power to oppose our genuine good.*

## What to Do When Unhappy

Here is what to do the next time you feel unhappy. *Don't label yourself as unhappy; instead, see yourself as confused about things.* This sets in motion an entirely different process, a healthy one. By calling yourself unhappy, you make yourself unhappy, for the naming produces the feeling. But if you will be unemotionally aware of your confusion, the thinking process of Supermind changes in your favor.

Your thinking might proceed like this: "Well, here I am in confusion. All right. But confusion need not mean unhappiness. I am not unhappy when baffled by a crossword puzzle; I go on to solve it. I can do likewise with this situation. I can study the principles of the Supermind to clear the air."

Earnestly try this. You will experience a wonder. It will be just as impossible for grief to occur as it was previously impossible for happiness to exist.

## How to Let Happiness Reveal Itself

Henry David Thoreau once wrote, *We are surrounded by a rich and fertile mystery. May we not probe it, pry into it, employ ourselves about it, a little?*

Here I will supply some clues for solving a mystery surrounding millions of unhappy people.

*You cannot know happiness in advance. Happiness must reveal itself from moment to moment.*

Only in the Outer World can you know things in advance. You know how the moon will affect the tides or you know that sugar will sweeten tea. They can be accurately forecast because they follow natural laws. But happiness cannot be known in advance. Please follow this.

Notice how you believe that you know what will bring happiness. Think of a few items. What are they? Success in an enterprise? Win back a loss? New surroundings? Next, notice what happened when you actually attained them on previous occasions. Were you any different or any happier? No, their attraction faded, leaving you as empty as you were before.

So it was not knowing at all, but only an assumption. But we forget, we always forget, that what we found was not the happiness we actually sought.

When you truly understand, you see that happiness must be permanently in you, regardless of the passing exterior show.

True happiness then is in whatever happens to you, not in what you prophesy *should* happen to you. It is being unwanted, as well as in getting a dozen invitations. It is in being plain-looking, as well as being handsome. It is in having nothing to depend upon, as well as having the supports of money and position.

Happiness is in everything and it is in nothing. It is only when we fail to see this that we fall out of harmony with the happiness already existing within.

Marcus Aurelius supplies a final clue: *You can remove out of the way many useless things which disturb you, for they lie entirely in your opinion toward them ....*

When the new view comes to you, words take on their esoteric meanings and will work to change your experience for the better in any situation. Let the following Supermind word associations guide your eternal progress:

*Love:* what is left when counterfeit love fades away

*Enlightenment:* to feel as well as know the truth

*Emotions:* powerful aids to self-awakening

*Conditioning:* outer influences affecting the mind

*Intelligence:* to admit the need for profound self-change

*Beauty:* to be a clear and sensible person

*Anger:* a defense against what we are unwilling to face

*Awakening:* the feeling of something entirely different

*Courage:* the determination to detect self-deception

*Happiness:* to come home to yourself

## Happiness Comes with Self-Unity

From a classic book entitled *The Walled Garden of Truth* comes this revealing idea: *As long as you have no self-unity, what difference does it make what you decide to do?*

I wonder whether you see the jewel hidden within these few words? There is something vital for your exploration. Here is what it means: As long as our choices are based on fleeting desires or on egotistical ambitions, no good can occur. Such desires and ambitions are like skyrockets which flash brilliantly for a moment, only to disappear into the darkness.

We can phrase this in another way: Whatever is done in a state of disunity will be wrong; that is, it contributes an empty thrill but never true satisfaction. But whatever is decided from our center of consciousness will be right; we make authentic gains.

Having absorbed this idea, do you see how it explains many of your activities? Suppose one day you feel unhappy and restless. You decide to relieve the uneasiness, so you do whatever occurs to you. It can be one of a thousand things. You go shopping, use the telephone, raid the refrigerator, talk to yourself, conduct business, walk someplace, talk to people and so on. It gets you nowhere because, wherever the self-split man goes, it is the wrong place. The cupboard is always bare. *We sense this, but we fear to stop running because we do not see that fullness is always here, never there.*

So it is utterly useless to decide anything at all while we are still self-divided.

So the only sensible task is to work at self-unity. Here is one way. Try to see attacks of heartache as selfish demands upon you. That is what they are. They demand your strength and time, your attention and your quietness, your very life itself. Never consent. Tell the attacks of grief and despondency that you have much better things to do with your time. Then refuse them the egotistical attention they crave. See all such onslaughts as big bluffs to be ignored, just as you would turn away from a yapping dog. Let me give you a deeper insight through a question and answer period after one of my lectures:

**Q:** I know that my question involves many avenues, but please supply a single answer. How can I be truly happy?

**A:** Accept defeat of all your fixed ideas as to what constitutes happiness. Let them be totally conquered. Know nothing about happiness. Now, a man rarely realizes his possession of fixed ideas, which he fiercely holds as valid, so he is unable to offer them up for sacrifice. Yet, every time you feel unhappy, you *do* see their falseness. They *force* you to see them. Accept the plain fact that you do not know what will make you happy. Now, you are on the way.

**Q:** You are right, of course, but I also see the great problem. I don't want defeat for my pet notions.

**A:** I know. But cheer up. The time will come when you see your defeat as the very victory you wish. Remember the prodigal son. By acknowledging defeat, he found his way home.

## Esoteric Truths About Happiness

1. The Supermind-way delivers true happiness under all circumstances.

2. Mere excitement is not authentic happiness.

3. Abandon all preconceived ideas about the happy, worldly life.

4. Refuse to live in fear and desperation.

5. Your interior cosmic self is free and happy already.

6. You need not painfully endure anything.

7. Apparent misfortune can be turned into psychic gold.

8. A sincere call for authentic aid attracts it.

9. It is cosmic intelligence to see through our pretenses.

10. Use Supermind principles to achieve self-unity with cosmic force.

# 11

# How New Supermind Energies Overcome Obstacles

A young prince was supplied with the secrets of a castle ruled over by his father, the king. Among them was the secret route for gaining admittance to the castle in case he should find himself outside during an enemy attack. The prince listened carefully, but in the excitement of daily castle life, his memory grew dim.

One day while he hunted, an enemy army besieged the castle. Wishing to return, the prince searched his memory. He realized that his only task was to clearly recall what he had once known so well. So combining thought with action, he went to work.

Reaching the moat, he remembered that it was necessary to swim directly beneath the drawbridge to the castle wall. Next, he recalled the hidden doorway at the base of the outer wall. Proceeding inside to the dungeon, he remembered where its key was hidden. So step by step, he passed beyond the obstacles to the safety of the inner castle.

We have forgotten the way back. But that is not a dreadful situation. Not at all. It is an opportunity for heroic adventure. So do not hesitate to risk failure. Be cheerfully willing to fail and fail. Eventually, you will see that there is no failure, only a false label of failure.

If you can find only 1 percent of valor in yourself and 99 percent timidity, that is just fine. Go ahead with just that much. To what little you have, more will be added.

Do not be discouraged in your efforts to use obstacles for spiritual growth. Remember two things: (1) The higher the barrier, the greater the opportunity for advancement. (2) You are never asked to do the impossible, which means it is possible to use and pass beyond every obstacle.

Make your plans for inner advancement and make yourself do them.

## The Facts About Self-Confidence

Here is how questions on attaining self-confidence can be answered:

**Q:** Please explain the coming and going of self-confidence. One minute I'm on the mountain top, the next I'm down.

**A:** What we ordinarily call self-confidence is not confidence at all. It is merely a temporary elation springing from a strong desire. When the desire is weakened by invasion by other desires, you feel downcast.

**Q:** How does it work in a practical situation?

**A:** You desire to go into business for yourself. Because the rewards seem great, you feel able to achieve your aim. But later, when problems arise, they promote new desires, like wanting to take it easier or wanting another goal which offers greater rewards. So you no longer feel self-confident toward your original goal.

**Q:** What, then, is authentic self-confidence?

**A:** You will know that when false confidence fades away.

When emotions feel blocked along the Supermind-trail, they transmit misleading messages of discouragement to the mind. The sleepy mind gullibly accepts the falsehoods as facts, and so cannot see how anything can be different. But it can. Let us leave the gullibility to those who wish to remain asleep.

The enlightened René Descartes taught, *To be possessed of an energetic mind is not enough; the first requirement is to use it correctly.*

Let's wisely start with something to be remembered always: Obstacles do not exist in bothersome people, nor in domestic or business difficulties, nor in past failures, nor in anything else like these. Every obstacle exists within ourselves. What gain to grasp this! In a flash you have narrowed your search down to the right place. You now know where to direct your energies for practical work.

But if obstacles are self-erected, the self can also do things differently. It can refuse to create them through wrong thinking. Take a man and woman with a strained and unnatural relationship. It is strained because their confused thinking goes like this: "In order to get what I think I want from you, I must give you what you think you want from me." Both end up miserable, for neither wants what they think they want. But if they lived in the Supermind, naturalness would enter the relationship.

We fall victim to self-defeating thoughts and actions only because we do not see them as self-defeating. In our confusion we even call them the exact opposite, such as labeling stubbornness as strength of character. You have known those who proudly declare, "No one tells me how to think!" That, of course, is fearful defensiveness, indicating weakness. The fact is, everyone tells such people how to think, though they are unaware of it. Someday, they must see that veracity is the only cure for whatever ails them.

Cheerfully realize that barriers and negativities are self-destroying. What a different man or woman you will be when you see this! When you quietly observe negativities, they flee from you, like foxes from an alert farmer.

You might be in the company of people when something is done or said that irritates you. You alertly watch the irritation as it rises and churns within. By appearing before the power of your awareness, its pseudo-power is weakened.

## Make Room for New Discoveries with Supermind

The road to the Supermind is a clearing process, much like ridding a stretch of desert of its rocks and bushes to make room for a highway. As the rocks of misinformation go from the mind, room is made for new discoveries which tell us what we want to know. What are these discoveries?

1. If we are not content without it, we will not be content with it.

2. *By permitting a confused society to tell us how to live, we also permit its confusion to punish us.*

3. The reason there is so much grief in the world is that neurosis is enormously aggressive; it is compelled to find targets.

4. *If we did not think we were unhappy, we would not be.*

5. No one can enjoy a truth for which he is unprepared, any more than an ape can appreciate a harp.

6. *If we will repeatedly suffer the humiliation of admitting that we really do not know what we are talking about, eventually we will.*

7. As stern as it sometimes appears to be, the truth is love and is never anything but love.

8. *Supermind-thinking alters and improves our outer acts quite naturally, just as a new tree influences and improves a barren yard.*

9. Freedom is in invisible guidance, not in visible aid.

10. *Genuine self-renewal begins the moment we earnestly inquire into the processes, tricks, illusions and powers of the mind.*

In order to change a man, spiritual facts must not be taken as dramatic sentiments. This common mistake is made by those with the urge to dramatize everything, especially themselves. By taking spiritual facts as practical pointers, there is no need for an exhausting stage performance. Deep down, every actor yearns to leave the stage and be himself.

*We discover what is truly important by courageously separating ourselves from everything providing a mere feeling of importance.*

The craving for new and exciting experiences prevents discovery of what is real within a man. Excitements are temporary, passing and disappointing, but what is real is forever. If we are not alert, the physical body can deceive us into thinking that we have changed, when in fact we have merely felt a strong sensation. That sensation will inevitably swing over to its opposite of dullness. There is another kind of excitement having no opposite. It is that of the Supermind.

There is one true gate and a thousand false gates. The gate to the Kingdom of Truth is wide open for anyone to enter, but there are no flashing lights or promising signs. It is perfectly plain, without allurements. It appeals only to what is real in a seeker, not to excitable desires. If the gate glitters with man-made ornaments, do not enter.

## Relaxation Is Your Natural State

George Gurdjieff observed that the world is not ruled by human beings, but by negative emotions inhabiting human beings. A glance at a newspaper is evidence enough.

Untamed emotions and personal frustration are as inseparable as children and noise. Using the emotions to straighten out a problem is like using an electric fan to straighten out papers on a desk. So our quest toward the Supermind must include a *new kind* of victory over reckless feelings.

179

It is a peculiar tragedy of human nature that a man will not give up the very negative emotions that wreck him. A woman once told me of her heavy pressures, attended by painful moods. I asked whether she would like to get rid of them. She angrily shouted, "No!" She meant it. We must investigate this strange situation.

A person refuses to give up his painful moods because he fears he would be empty without them. Notice this for yourself. Notice how painful feelings, like a sense of loss or indignation, provide a peculiar exhilaration. They induce a false sense of aliveness.

We must be willing to give up this counterfeit aliveness if we are to have the real thing. Gurdjieff again remarks that the last thing a man will give up is his suffering.

When enemy emotions fail to destroy a man, they themselves are destroyed, like an attacking soldier who falls back from a high wall.

The history of World War I records the tragic error of the British armored cruiser, *Black Prince*. In the darkness and confusion of battle, it fell in with the German fleet, thinking it was British. It discovered its mistake only when the Germans blasted and sank it. That is what happens when we unconsciously associate with enemy emotions, taking them as friends.

All forms of negativity are unconscious. Because they operate like thieves in the night, we are unaware of them. This applies to harmful emotions like discouragement and self-pity. We rise above them through conscious awareness of their presence. Consciousness has wings.

Let's see how this connects with physical and emotional tension. Awareness is certain to make you feel healthier. Catch yourself at odd moments with a clenched jaw or tense hands. Simply be aware of the tension. Now, you don't really need to *do* anything, you need only *cease* doing something. You need only let go. Physical tension, like psychic tension, is nothing more than an unnecessary absence of your natural state of relaxation.

You need not add to your already complete true self and cannot add to a non-existent false self. So why not relax?

## The World Offers Itself to You

Let's connect natural awareness with chronic feelings of tiredness, a common complaint of physically healthy people. To do this we must frankly glance at a vital teaching of Supermind: Nothing is more tiring than the dreadful human habit of fakery. Schopenhauer expressed it in the following manner:

> *People are like the moon ... they show you only one of their sides. Every man has an innate talent for mimicry, or making a mask ... so that he can always look as if he really were what he pretends to be ... and its effect is extremely deceptive.*

Be authentic and you will be almighty. Only an eagle can perch safely on top of the cliff.

We must see the difference between temporary relief from emotional distress and healthy insight into it. A fisherman in a leaky boat would not be content with bailing out the water day after day. He would search out and repair the cause of the trouble. So must we look at causes, not effects. A businessman is hurt and angry over a financial venture that falls through. By shaking his head to the suggestion that it has power to disturb, he retains self-command. A woman worries that life is passing her by. By living from her central self, not her conditioned mind, she is fulfilled every day.

Let neither circumstance nor person tell you how to feel. Tell yourself.

Don't slap labels on your feelings. Don't mechanically call one feeling good and another bad; don't name one emotion as happy and another as depressing. The very act of labeling throws your feelings into a whirlpool of confusion, like clothes in a swirling washing machine. Instead, be silently aware of the feeling. Don't call it anything at all. This keeps you out of the whirlpool. It retains quietness in your Inner World, regardless of events in the Outer World.

Feelings function normally when you live from the principles of the Supermind. Take the idea of winning good things for yourself as an example. Never assume what your added good will be. Never assume how and when it will come. Assumptions are projections of your own desires, which produce nothing new. Your added good is *always* different from your preconceived imaginations. It is an item on a higher shelf previously reached. The new cannot be assumed. To assume what it means you already know what it is. It is like sending a present to yourself and pretending surprise.

Life wants to give you new and good things. But you must chase nothing. You need only be receptive to whatever chases you. Live from the Supermind. Then, a new world has no choice but to offer itself to you.

*Like draws to like, and the goods which belong to you gravitate to you.* (Emerson)

## How to Realize the Priceless Present Moment

How would you feel if this were the very first day of your life? That's the whole idea! You would enjoy it with freshness. Having no past conditioning to blur your feelings, you would respond perfectly to everything. You would and could not know dread or defensiveness.

Live from moment to moment, just as if every new moment is all there is. For that, in truth, is all there is.

This brings us to the mystical meaning of *time*.

When you enjoy the present moment, you do not worry about tomorrow's enjoyment. True enjoyment is all-inclusive. It is only when you fail to enjoy the present that you seek escape into yesterday or tomorrow. But there is no escape into either, for neither exists. Because there is only now, enjoyment is now or never. Memorize these words — *Now is new.*

Smash the tyranny of the past and future by constantly tugging yourself back to the here and now. Be conscious of yourself at this very moment, even as you hold this book. In that state you are receptive to true inspiration. If your telephone rings, you need to be home to answer it.

We rob ourselves of the priceless present moment whenever we absently assume that we will be happier an hour, week or year from now. Time as measured by the calendar has nothing whatsoever to give you. Happiness through the mere passage of days is a dreadful delusion, which unthinking man rarely unmasks. *You*, your psychological self, must be different in February than you were in January. You can change February all right, but February cannot change you.

To attribute magic to calendar time is like believing that the rising sun can of itself transform a shack into a palace. No, something else is required — a builder.

You are that builder. Do not be afraid to know absolutely nothing of how you are to behave in the next minute, day, year. The unknown, which appears so frightening, is your very fullness. Jesus stated it as simply as possible: *Let not your heart be troubled.*

I will supply a test of inner understanding. Ask, "What shall I do with my life?" If you hear no answer, if you remain in the dark, yet remain calm and unconcerned, you can join the select circle of awakened men. However, let us proceed further:

**Q:** You seem to say that there is no use in thinking of ways to be happy.

**A:** It is pointless to pursue customary methods for happiness. When you are actually happy, do you think about it in any way at all? No. It is just there; you simply live it out without thought. Only when you are unhappy do you think about happiness. This proves that contentment exists only when we don't try to bring it about.

**Q:** I have a family problem. Why can't I use my usual thinking to solve it?

**A:** Usual thinking is the very cause of problems, but people don't see it. Using your conditioned mind to clear the problem is like trying to clean a cup with a muddy rag. Nothing works but Supermind-thinking.

**Q:** In one of your talks, you stressed the value of thinking clearly toward ourselves. I want to do this.

**A:** Start by realizing that all thoughts about yourself consist of memories only. *You* are not these memories. Therefore, you are not bad because you once broke the law, and you are not good because you showed up one day at church. You, at this very moment, are totally pure. By seeing this, you think clearly and live freely.

## How Cosmic and Psychic Energies Are Awakened

Here is an obstacle to avoid: Do not mistake *hearing* for *understanding*. After hearing lectures or reading books on esotericism, people assume they understand. This assumption blocks the penetration of an understanding which is capable of stirring sleeping energies. A motorist would not endlessly study a map of the Grand Canyon. He would let the absorbed information activate him into moving forward to the canyon itself. So does the sincere student first understand, then permit his new knowledge to roll him toward discoveries.

Humility helps. Humility is often mistaken for weakness, but true humility is nothing of the sort. It is a type of receptivity which builds psychic strength. The *Tao-Teh-King* explains that a great river attains greatness by being lower than the dozens of streams flowing into it.

Have no doubt, you will receive fresh psychic energies when you have actually and factually made room for them. One way to make room is to want them more than you want anything else. Higher energies will not share the same room with lower desires. It is supremely important that your foremost wish is for strengths of the Supermind. Here is why. An insincere call for help attracts insincere helpers, while a genuine call attracts genuine aid.

When new energies come, do not hold them in reserve. Never save your intelligence, cheerfulness or anything else for tomorrow. Enjoy and exhaust them in the present moment. A tree withholding its natural fruit soon loses its fruitfulness, but the benevolent tree develops greater capacities.

Advancement comes when we cease to do certain things, for example:

Don't carry the false burden of another person's bad behavior. Don't allow another to shift his responsibility and guilt onto your back. A weak person always tries to do this. Become aware and quietly refuse, for your sake and his. Marcus Aurelius makes it clear in the following words: *He who does wrong, does wrong against himself.* The ill-behaved person must bear full responsibility, otherwise he cannot learn. A false sense of sentimental sympathy toward him only increases his inner chaos. Every man must race to his own rescue.

What about your duties toward others? Some systems make the most of this to exploit the gullible. You can be sure that those who love to preach about giving and sharing expect to be on the receiving end. They reward the unwary with a mere *self-picture* of being generous and charitable, while picking their pockets. What a gigantically cruel hoax.

You have no duty to give anything to another that you have not first given to yourself. In fact, we cannot give virtue unless we first possess it, any more than an empty pitcher can give water. Place first things *first*. Suspend the idea of giving virtuous things to another; work to reveal your own hidden treasures. Here we have one of those very difficult situations. Men avoid such self-revelation because they assume they already have true goodness. They also avoid self-discovery because it is much easier to dream than work. But the sincere seeker is tired of nightmares; he wants to wake up.

## Come Back to Yourself the Cosmic Way

When it comes to agriculture, man is wise. Over the centuries, he has cultivated the fruits of the field while removing the weeds. Consequently, we have finer fruits.

Psychologically, it is another story. He waters the weeds, neglects the fruits and wonders at his poverty!

Over the years I have found the same kind of psychic weeds growing in the mental gardens of those who fail; psychic weeds such as fear of the new and unknown, mental laziness, refusal to use pain for gain, dishonesty, lack of persistence, ignorance of spiritual facts, shallow values, hardened attitudes, pride, imitation of hypocritical society, insincerity, influence of negative people and unawareness of psychic hypnosis.

All of these can be rooted out, once and for all. Take the fear of the new and unknown. A fisherman seeking refuge from a storm steered his boat into a nearby bay. A friendly villager put him up for the night in a room next to a fragrant rose garden. He could not sleep. By placing a sack of fish near the pillow, he slept soundly.

We are like that. Our familiarity with the lesser makes us uncomfortable with the greater. The fragrant life for which we yearn is wrongly seen as a threat. Because of our blurred psychic vision, we mistake friend for enemy.

Or take unawareness of being in a state of psychic sleep. Here is a good example of this:

We are asleep whenever we let the body move ahead while the mind lingers behind. The body crosses a busy street, while the mind remains in place, hypnotized by an event of a moment or a month ago. This leaves the individual unaware of what is happening in the here and now. Such unconsciousness leads to weakness and accidents.

Snap the spell. Snap it now. Become aware of what happens *as* it happens. Notice the expression on that man's face, the tone of your voice, the color of that teacup, the position of your left arm, that flashing thought. Bring yourself back to yourself. There is good reason for it. Follow the guidance contained in the conversation below:

**Q:** Do physical changes result from absorbing *Supermind* ideas?

**A:** Profound physical changes, for they are promoted by new inner causes. You walk, talk, tilt your head differently and so on. Your body is more comfortable, attractive, healthy, energetic. But remember, they must happen spontaneously, as you welcome newness. If the false self tries to create them, it will only be the switching of one artificiality for another.

**Q:** How do terms like *faith* and *belief* connect with *Supermind* teachings?

**A:** The only valid belief is one which you prove personally by a loftier life. But when this happens, the words no longer have meaning. Words are labels, and you cannot describe an inner certainty; you just taste it. How would you describe to someone the taste of a peach?

**Q:** Why am I so worried that a future event may not turn out as I want?

**A:** You are concerned because your false sense of self connects it with a false need, like the need to impress others. You fear losing the artificial aliveness you get from impressing others. For instance, you hope your talk before the club will make you seem important. When the false need to be important melts away, so does worry.

## Dare to Ask Questions

Never hesitate to voice your doubts about anything along the Supermind trail. Get your bewilderments out in front of your psychic sight. Look them over, just as if they are as solid as rocks. I know many people who hesitate to ask certain questions, fearing they may sound shocking or foolish. And sometimes they worry that no answer exists. You need not hide your doubts. Nothing is being hidden from you. The answer to every question is ready for the asking. There is only one requirement: You must not resist the answer merely because it goes against your present beliefs.

You wonder at the existence of so many weird human doctrines? *The world is a huge hospital where every patient thinks he's a doctor.*

You worry over your fate if you should ever run out of the strength to push and plan your way along? *It is amazing how easily the earth spins in the universe without human thought.*

You cannot see how there can be anything else but your present day circumstances? *You cannot see the distant ocean while still standing in the desert.*

You helplessly feel yourself at the mercy of chance? *The feeling exists only in your acquired beliefs, not at all in actuality.*

You want to love and be loved? *Of course you do, but you wrongly connect love with a person or object, when in truth it is an inner energy.*

It is a sign of growing psychic maturity to ask questions you never dared to ask before as a certain person asked me in the following conversation:

**Q:** I am very much interested in your approach to the problem of suffering, but don't understand it. You say we must use sorrow to end sorrow. How?

**A:** Suffer voluntarily and consciously. Don't resist it. Face the pain in your unconscious parts in order to bring it up to consciousness.

**Q:** Can you illustrate this?

**A:** You feel like escaping nervousness, so you run a mental movie of a past pleasure. Don't. Face the anxiety with an adventurous spirit. Do this even if you don't grasp its value as yet. It awakens you.

**Q:** But why shouldn't I indulge in mental movies of a past or anticipated pleasure? What is wrong with this kind of stimulation?

**A:** It prevents awareness of genuine happiness found in the here and now. Tell me, do you prefer to *temporarily dream* about happiness or to *permanently experience* it?

## How to Get Satisfying Flavor from Life

Imagine yourself seated at the dinner table about to select a dessert. Before you are the choices of chocolate cake, apple pie or tapioca pudding. You select the cake but are dismayed to find it tasteless. Sampling the pie and the pudding, you find them also to be without flavor. As appealing as they *look*, they are flat, dull, disappointing. To eat them would not be pleasure but monotony.

Such is the condition of life without the flavor of accurate truth.

Flavor! That is the perfect word to describe the difference between mechanical movement and spontaneous flowing.

I will tell you a great secret. There is a flavor of life which you do not know as yet, but which awaits your receptivity. Do not think these are mere words. Their esoteric meaning is what you have been searching for all your life. There is an ancient saying, *He who tastes, knows.*

The trouble is we are not bold enough. With the right kind of boldness, former things pass away, and all things become new.

Now we must grasp something extremely important. *The facts that change us are not flavorful the first time we taste them.* Don't forget this. It will help you break down your resistance to beneficial principles.

We have already seen why esoteric truths are untasty at first. The false self suspects its own destruction and, therefore, dislikes the truth. Wanting to keep a man in psychic shipwreck, the artificial self throws all its deceit and anger and scorn against the invading facts.

If you eat a sour pickle, then eat a sweet orange, the orange will at first taste sour. But as you continue to eat the orange, its natural sweetness comes through. This is why persistence is essential to the spiritual seeker. It takes time to get rid of the sour which distorts the sweet.

We have seen the limitations of language in explaining the Supermind, which must be personally experienced. So to understand the similarity of certain words used in this book will be helpful.

To be aware means the same as being awake. Living in liberation is living in love. To be in a state of self-understanding is to be free of chronic grief. Being happy means the same as being a conscious human being. To taste the flavor of truth is the same as tasting authentic peace of mind.

In ancient legend, a hero named Peredur obtained an extraordinary stone which made him invisible. With his new power, he conquered a monster which was terrorizing a palace. So can we, by uniting with the unique Supermind, awaken new energies and overcome obstacles.

## Outstanding Ideas for Review

1. Use obstacles and frustrations in your cosmic path for inner advancement with Supermind.

2. Nothing is more loving than the truth itself.

3. Self-renewal begins as we study our own minds and free them from conditioned thinking.

4. Worldly excitements are temporary, but truth is forever.

5. Relaxation in Supermind is an exalted state you can attain.

6. Your true self can be made to reflect calmness, contentment and completeness at all times.

7. Life wants to give you new and good things.

8. Live only in the eternal NOW.

9. New psychic energies will enter you as you make room for them.

10. Overcome the spell of self-hypnosis with Supermind's power.

# 12

## Secrets Treasures
## of the Supermind

Suppose you have attended the theater. The play comes to an end and you prepare to leave. The hour is late; you want to go home. But suddenly, an actor leaps onstage, clad in a Shakespearian costume. Demanding your attention, he goes into a long and dull performance.

You really don't want to give him your attention, but the seat is comfortable, it's a long trip home, and so you remain where you are. But as you sit, you somehow feel that you are in the wrong place.

The actor finally exits, so once more you get ready to leave. But another actor, a fortune-teller, rushes onstage to insist that you stay and watch him. He solemnly announces his power to predict your future. You are in no mood for it, but there is something disturbingly compelling about his personality. Against your own better judgment, you let him talk you into watching his performance. Vaguely restless, you sit and listen to a batch of vague prophecies, which you sense are phony.

By the time the fortune-teller exits, you are utterly weary. You desperately want to go home. As you start to rise, a third actor pops out to demand your attention. But you have had enough. That's all! No more! You walk out and go home.

*In life, the bad actors are the thousands of senseless thoughts that pop onto the stage of your mind.* Selfishly, they demand your time and attention, while leaving you bored and restless. Observe for yourself how this is so. Notice how this worry or that nervousness distracts you from your quiet psychic home.

You need not remain a captive audience of these preposterous performers. You can get up and walk out as soon as you *see through them.* The secrets of the Supermind enable you to do so.

## You Are Wiser Than You Think

How deeply will you dig in order to expose and destroy a false sense of self? At that same depth will you know genuineness. It is like digging away sandy soil in order to build on solid rock.

Yes, there will be dry seasons when you feel that it is just too much, that you have worked too long and too hard without reward. The discouragement is intensified by the desire to go back to your former lower level, but you know you can never go back. You feel utterly trapped, like a passenger who has left the sinking ship but who has not as yet sighted land.

Never mind. You are doing just fine. Even if you don't understand, there is something that does.

Here is the esoteric secret for clarifying a confused mind: Live with the confusion, without resistance, until it destroys itself.

You are not only wiser than you think, but you *know* that you are wiser. That is the reason why a man in trouble fights against the very cosmic facts that could save him. His insight is the very reason he argues. His false self tries to protect its false position, like a thief tries to prevent the police from taking his stolen goods.

Let your Supermind think for you.

There is a curious feature about gaining the insight of Supermind. Before gaining it, we were certain we already understood. But when winning true insight, we see that we knew nothing. It can be compared with the great wisdom we thought we had as teenagers! There is a Sufi saying, *Until copper becomes gold, it does not know that it was copper.* In other words, we do not realize that we were asleep until we begin to awaken.

Let me pass on to you a seldom realized feature about human nature. Your understanding will explain many mysteries and supply new solutions.

A man thinks he is a single, unified individual, but he is not. He has dozens of different selves within him, many of them contradictory to others. Self A takes over, is replaced a moment later by Self B, which in turn is replaced by Self C. We usually refer to this as a change in mood or attitude, but it is helpful to see it as the temporary domination of one self over the others. A man says something he thinks is clever, but later regrets it. Two selves were involved. A woman is highly enthusiastic over a project today, but abandons it tomorrow. This is because two contradictory selves were in charge on different days.

Man fails to see these contradictory selves, consequently, he is torn left and right in confusion and error. It is as if a dozen seamen claimed in turn to be the captain of a ship. One grabs the wheel and turns the ship south, but he is knocked aside by another claimant who switches to north. Each grabs the wheel only long enough to be shoved away. No wonder the ship gets nowhere!

But self-union is possible. Everything in this book works for self-captaincy through self-unity. Start by being aware of disunity. See it clearly in yourself. Your awareness of the confusion will restore your clear command.

## A New Look at Morality with Supermind

The Supermind leads us into an entirely different sense of goodness. We do not ascend to it by following man-made doctrines, much less by mechanically practicing exterior virtues commonly applauded by society. Such public preachings have no more power for psychic elevation than a traffic law has power to make a motorist a good driver. Jesus warned repeatedly against a surface morality, with hidden hypocrisy.

Unawakened people are victims of their public virtues. I don't know anything more painful than trying to be "good." And I don't know anything more to be avoided than "good" people; they are so bad. *And be on guard against the good and just! They would crucify those who devise their own virtue* .... (Nietzsche)

Man-made moralities can only keep human perversity in check, and when relaxed, as in warfare, we quickly see the difference between commanded goodness and true virtue arising from cosmic conscience. The unawakened individual maintains a surface goodness only because certain vices have no appeal for him anyway or because he fears the consequences of disobeying public tastes in morality. A morality based in fear is deeply immoral.

But the self-unified man has no such thing as suspended goodness; he is good simply because it cannot occur to him to be anything else. Only an awakened man is truly moral.

It is a wicked world, far worse than realized. As Erasmus points out in his classic book, *The Praise of Folly*, it is a world where fools are honored by other fools. And as John Acton remarks, *All great men are bad.*

We must clearly see human badness as it is, unhampered by sentimentality or by subtle projections of our own false sense of goodness. Once seen, we are free from the harm of badness. To really see it means we are no longer part of it. We do not see the depth of badness in others because we do not first see it in ourselves. We live in dream-pictures of being pleasant, noble and loving, while underneath we conceal some dreadful dragons. But awareness of our own badness sets us free, thus freeing us from others.

Once free, we do not condemn the world's evil, but clearly understand it. We forgive others because we have first forgiven ourselves.

Human wickedness results from man's psychic hypnosis and from his ignorance of his true nature. The only solution is for each individual to shake himself awake.

## How Falseness Disappears with Supermind

Let us conduct a short question and answer period as to how Supermind hobbles sin and evils as follows:

**Q:** How, then, does *Supermind* define sin and evil?

**A:** Sin is anything false and unreal. To state differently, it is any self-defeating action performed under psychic hypnosis. By living from the false self, instead of Supermind, we do foolish things. As the inner light dawns and as we live from our true nature, falseness and wickedness disappear. Then, a man becomes good in every sense of the word. He becomes sane, decent, pleasant.

**Q:** But does evil really exist?

**A:** It does and it doesn't. Don't let this seeming contradiction bother you. You may think you see a wicked cobra about to strike, but where is the wickedness when you see it was only a piece of rope? Upon awakening, evil vanishes from man.

**Q:** How can we awaken from our own badness?

**A:** It changes before your very eyes by quietly observing it without moralization. That is one thing you must never do — never indulge in shallow moralizations. If you see your badness and imagine you must be good, you are painfully torn between the two. Quiet awareness, without condemnation, destroys human ideas of both bad and good. Then, you are free of conflict.

Do not be afraid of the difficulties along the way. And do not fight anything, such as your depressions, blunders, despairs or your badness. "Resist not evil." *The one thing evil cannot stand is for you to quietly observe it in yourself without self-condemnation, without panic and without fight.*

A man can be activated by negative forces, yet not *be* them in essence. He must work to understand that they have no power in themselves, only that which is carelessly allowed. He pays the penalty of self-division only because he fails to take proper care of himself.

What a man, when the inner and the outer are one!

Freedom from negativity is attained through a strange but certain process. We must first be aware of the negative item, perhaps hostility, before we can see its non-connection with the real self. As a first step, therefore, the hostility must be quietly observed, not suppressed, denied, rationalized or even condemned. After that, we must cease identification with it, we must not call it our own. In unawareness, we call it our own, and so fall under its power. But awareness without personalization carries us into the clear, like a ship breaking through fog.

As I said, the process is strange. We must see how terrible we are in order to see how terrible we are not!

Awareness of any negativity within us is first unseen, then perceived, then shocking and then liberating.

# How to Discover Your
# Secret Kingdom of Supermind

What a situation! Here is a man possessing the priceless privileges of the Supermind, yet failing to use them for his own advantage. He lives with a haunted mind that could, with right effort, be transformed into a brilliant guiding light.

If only he would pause in his wonderment at the universe of starry skies and wonder at the vast universe within his own mind.

If only he would discover his secret kingdom!

Does this secret kingdom, where all is well, really exist? Yes. You may not be aware of it, but it does exist. Let's hear about it from four men who were widely separated from each other by time and space, but who came to the same enlightenment.

Count Leo Tolstoy admits the skepticism of his early years, and then testifies to his great discovery of the kingdom as follows:

*I knew not the light, and I thought there was no sure truth in life; but when I perceived that only light enables men to live, I sought to find the sources of the light .... And when I reached this source of light I was dazzled with its splendor, and I found there full answers to my questions as to the purpose of the lives of myself and others ....*

The Eastern wisdom of Shankara reminds us of how the kingdom is attained with the following words:

*The realization of Truth is brought about by perception, and not in the least by ten millions of acts.*

Chuang-tse, the teacher of Taoism, happily observes in the following that dwellers in the secret kingdom always know what to do:

*He who knows the Tao is sure to be well acquainted with the principles that appear in the procedures of things. Acquainted with those principles, he is sure to understand how to regulate his conduct in all varying circumstances. Having that understanding, he will not allow things to injure him.*

Ralph Waldo Emerson offers a gentle invitation to come and live in the secret kingdom with these words:

*We are very near to greatness: one step and we are safe: can we not take the leap?*

What kind of man leaps to true greatness? The one with the intense intention to take the leap regardless of everything. The person who has caught his first glimpse of that strange *something else* is like a man in a dark passageway. Just ahead is a tiny glimpse of light, so faint that he often doubts his own eyes, yet he stumbles ahead. He will be attacked by loneliness and despondency, he will run out of breath, he will wonder whether it is all worthwhile, but he cannot stop. He is urged on by the inner whispering that he is heading in the right direction at last. He realizes that his only responsibility is to keep his eyes toward the light, for the light itself never wavers. And so he finds his way to that light.

And so it is with anyone. Whoever is eager enough to find the secret kingdom will never fail in his quest.

## Twelve Words That Can Work Magic For You

If you become confused at times in working out human relations, the following points brought out might aid you:

**Q:** I am suddenly aware of how disappointed we all are in each other. Why don't we simply choose to be nice, instead of disappointing?

**A:** Your confusion stems from assuming that a man could behave differently if only he chose to do so. He cannot. An unawakened man has no more choice of behavior than a cat can help acting like a cat. He is *compelled* to act out his present nature. To behave differently, he must wake up.

**Q:** You say he has no power of choice, but doesn't he choose to behave badly?

**A:** No, not even that. He does everything mechanically and unconsciously.

**Q:** But what motivates his actions?

**A:** The dominating desire of the moment. Whatever desire arises, he is compelled to follow it. There is no choice in desire. A man thinks he makes a choice and then takes charge of it, when in fact a desire springs up which takes charge of *him*. An unfree mind cannot behave differently. Observe all this in yourself. It makes you different.

A painting by the English mystical artist William Blake is called *Vain Desire*. It shows a man attempting to reach the stars with a ladder. Here is a reminder of the futility of trying to reach celestial regions with wrong desires.

One such wrong desire, as we have seen, is the wish to have others tell us what to do. No one can tell you what is right for you except yourself. So start telling yourself what to do. If you blunder for ten years while thinking for yourself, that is rich treasure when compared with living these ten years under the mental domination of another. The only true, honest and enriching authority is the internal authority of your own Supermind. *Be ye lamps unto yourselves; be ye a refuge to yourselves. Betake yourselves to no external refuge.* (Buddha)

Another vain desire is the seeking of strange psychical experiences, such as mind-reading and foretelling the future. Do not desire them as they are not your goal. Your aim is much higher than that. Many true teachers, including William Law, an Englishman, were strangers to such things. Your aim, so utterly pure, is to be a happy, healthy, balanced man or woman. Simplify the whole business by saying with Emerson, *I wish to be a true and free man ....*

How can we tell a false desire from a true one? Well, just about the best way is to actually obtain what you want. If it is false and if you watch closely, you will see that you are no different or happier than you were before.

In just 12 words I can tell you how to turn the next hour into pure magic. ***Place the truth that you know before the desire that you feel.***

## The Sure Cure for Loneliness

Of all sad words uttered by men and women, there are no sadder ones than, "It is the utter loneliness I cannot bear; the nagging, desolating loneliness." And not just a few add, "No one seems to care whether I come or go."

Lonely people are usually advised to head off in the

direction of new friends and activities. But this advice is supplied by those who have never really come face to face with their own sense of isolation. It is easy for a rich man to tell the poor that money isn't everything.

Certainly, friends and activities have their place in maintaining a balanced life. We are simply saying they are no good for solving the problem of loneliness, for they have no power to do so. All they can do is distract you from the gnawing for awhile. And when you come back to your own mind, which you always must, there it is again. It is always there again, isn't it? So this is a clue: Loneliness exists in the mind and nowhere else. This is our starting point for the Supermind solution.

You are alone. Nothing happens. The telephone doesn't ring and the mailman passes you by. You have only yourself for company. Now, this aloneness cannot translate itself into loneliness unless the mind carelessly does so. If, when alone, you do not permit the unconscious mind to mechanically label the state as loneliness, the feeling of isolation cannot arise. It is the unconscious labeling or naming that causes the trouble by activating the feelings.

It is the non-labeling of the state that keeps it pure and prevents its defilement. The way to prove it is to test it every time you feel lonely. You will finally see that Supermind-thinking makes loneliness absolutely impossible.

If you see a figure in a white sheet and do not call it a ghost, but see it only as a figure in a white sheet, you will not be scared. The non-naming prevents all the associative thoughts of fear about the word "ghost" from arising.

Loneliness persists, even when surrounded by others, because we call it frightening and then try to escape from the fright. But loneliness cannot be escaped because there is no such thing as loneliness; there is only an illusion created by false reactions. You can no more escape an illusion than you can escape from being chased by a non-existent tiger. You can, however, turn around and see there is really nothing there. Then, of course, you cease pointless attempts to escape.

Knowing this, Spinoza wrote, ... *I saw that all things which occasioned me any anxiety or fear had in themselves nothing of good or evil, except in so far as the mind was moved by them ....*

## How to Profit from Solitude

Seeing that aloneness need not mean loneliness, we can go on to discover rich rewards from solitude. The first is introduced by Arthur Schopenhauer as follows: *Really good society is everywhere of necessity very small. In brilliant festivals and noisy entertainments, there is always, at bottom, a sense of emptiness prevalent. A false tone is there ....*

Aloneness stops the drainage of our vital forces by human influences. It permits the mind to concentrate on what is essential to itself. Society in general and negative persons in particular always try to drain strength from those seeking higher ground. Be aware of this psychological process. A lower and weaker level always seeks a free ride from a higher and stronger level. It is against the law to permit weak people to steal your strength. Never permit it.

Use those times when you are all by yourself to reflect upon the principles of the Supermind. You have a fine opportunity to turn ideas into experience. Take the matter of health. It is only in recent years that the general public has understood the strong influence of the mind upon the body. Yet, thousands of years ago, the connection between ill health and psychic disorder was clearly revealed by Epicurus. He became famed as a healer when patients at his sanatoriums at Athens and Mytilene were restored to good health and cheery spirits. So use your reflective periods to connect yourself with universal principles.

To have only yourself for company is a great revelation. It is the perfect opportunity to see yourself as you are. You can then turn that self-knowledge into practical aims. I once spoke with a woman who admitted how easily her feelings were hurt by others. I asked her, "Do you see that you permit others to tell you how to feel? Why do you abandon your emotions to the influence of others?" The expression crossing her face indicated insight into her problem. Had she used her reflective periods for greater self-education, she could have saved herself years of distress.

Aloneness is a wise teacher. It reveals old weaknesses, but delivers new strengths. It puts us at ease with ourselves in all circumstances. Danish philosopher Soren Kierkegaard remarked that one sign of spiritual maturity was the ability to be comfortable when alone.

Finally, aloneness proves that we are never really alone after all. We are One with the whole of Life, in Supermind.

## The Supermind Way to Genuine Power

There is true power and there is false. While false power cleverly resembles the true, fooling millions, it is entirely destructive. It is like the difference between a real loaf of bread and a picture of a loaf. Because men and women do not understand this, they try to feed on false power, resulting in spiritual malnutrition.

False power originates in the false self, from the unnatural and unenlightened nature of man. It is power for harm.

True power has its source in the Supermind, from the non-human forces in the universe. It is power for good.

We can briefly review the nature of weakness — false power — in human beings. Weakness has an endless need to attack and defend. That is its entire operation — attack and defend, attack and defend. A weak person often gives the surface appearance of strength, but crumbles beneath the slightest challenge. He is like a rider tossed wildly about by a bucking bronco, while indignantly insisting that he is in charge.

The false self has no power whatsoever to clear up a life. But people do not realize this and, consequently, fail and fail without knowing why. An illusory self cannot do real work. It takes real bread to satisfy hunger.

Incidentally, attacking and defending accounts for much of the emotional exhaustion we see in people. When you are genuinely strong, you neither attack nor defend and so retain your energy.

When you see that the cosmic force of the entire universe is on the side of the liberated man, you can defy the world's falseness and get away with it in perfect safety. Begin by realizing the existence of the universal cosmic force within yourself.

Until this is understood, life must remain powerless and frustrating. To state it positively, when this is grasped, life becomes purposeful and satisfying for the first time. Consider these thoughts about new power the Supermind way:

1. Place yourself on your own side.

2. *You attract or repel according to your psychic radiations.*

3. It is a brave thing to know your need for new guidance and come right out with a request for it.

4. *Stop wasting your powers by imaginatively defending yourself against accusations not actually made.*

5. Whatever is natural is powerful.

6. *A state of weakness is perfect for you, providing you let it be filled with something other than your usual strengths.*

7. The truth alone can say, "I will never leave you."

8. *One sure sign of a breakthrough is that you would not go back to the old ways for anything on earth.*

9. You have it made when you don't care whether you have it made or not.

10. *Persistence prevails, like a stream that is temporarily blocked by boulders and then collects force enough to overflow onward.*

## How to Rise Above the Confusion of Opposing Compulsions

In my classes and lectures I often answer my listeners' questions in the following manner:

**Q:** I don't want to sound complaining, but why do I have so many bad breaks?

**A:** What you call your bad breaks are not at all what you assume they are. Your thinking must change. Having a negative response to an event, you assume the negativity is in the event when it is only in your negative response. But you don't see this. By breaking your habitual negativity, the same events could happen, but would not be seen as bad breaks.

**Q:** You mean they would appear as good fortune?

**A:** No. If you call one thing good, you must call its opposite bad. If you think it wonderful to make a big profit in your business, you will also think it terrible if you incur a large loss. The idea is to live above the opposites.

**Q:** I don't understand.

**A:** It is important that you do. To illustrate, suppose you are caught between two battling armies. You think Army A is friendly, but as you approach, it fires on you. You try Army B, but it also attacks. Army A then appears friendly for awhile, but suddenly turns on you again. So you confusedly stagger back and forth between the two, not knowing which is on your side. You finally realize that neither army is for you and this creates panic, for you have no allies at all. At that critical moment, you catch hold of a passing helicopter, which carries you far above both battling armies.

**Q:** But what *is* this state above the battle?

**A:** When you rise above it, you will see.

The reader can refer to the section in Chapter 2 entitled *Why We Must Go Beyond Human Thought* for a review of this useful secret of esotericism.

We must learn to look in the right direction. A miner searching for gold does not look toward the clouds for what is at his boots. Neither should we. The gold of life is here, not there.

So let your mind inquire into itself. We acquire knowledge from others, wisdom from ourselves. Supermind gives you knowledge which you can, by the magic power of receptivity, transform into guiding wisdom.

Be an independent investigator. To be by yourself, separate from others, provides one of the richest opportunities possible. It is the opportunity to be yourself!

How true are you to yourself? That is the degree of your contentment. *A happy life is one which is in accordance with its own nature.* (Seneca)

And with self-harmony comes a quiet beauty. We enjoy beauty only when we don't chatter about it, either mentally or orally. Bursting out in rapture over a pink sunset distracts us from appreciation, for our words are walls. Beauty is within a silent oneness with the beautiful.

## Summary of Valuable Secrets

1. You need not be a captive of useless and random thoughts.

2. The grand cosmic secret is to abandon a false sense of self.

3. You are much wiser than you think.

4. Simple awareness of badness brings about goodness.

5. You are very near to greatness, so take the leap.

6. Set the truth you know before the desire you feel.

7. Permit no one to drain your psychic strength.

8. Let solitude be your wise teacher.

9. True power has its source in the Supermind.

10. Let your mind inquire into itself and power its flight into Cosmic Truth with Supermind.

# 13

## How to Be Free of Pressures and Live Serenely

By thinking from your Supermind, you think without tension. When you live by the river, you don't wait anxiously for rain. Picture an inexperienced explorer lost in the jungles of the Amazon. In his panic he races left and right, tripping, clawing, falling, stunning himself. Realizing he is getting nowhere, he thinks, "Well, maybe I'm not running hard enough. I'd better double my speed." So he runs twice as fast and, of course, falls twice as hard.

That is typical of inaccurate reasoning which must be calmly set aside. *Effort in itself means nothing.* If we do wrong things and work harder, we merely do more wrong things. If effort alone could succeed, it would succeed. Even a small right effort produces right results.

The point is we must not work harder but work correctly. We must completely stop working wrongly. Right and wrong work cannot go together at the same time; it is one or the other. This is cosmic law.

Have the daring to stop doing things you really don't want to do. Can you see them? Look closely. Can you observe the many things you do because you reluctantly feel you *should* or *must?* Watch closely. Examine every action and reaction. Do you act naturally or do you act because you feel compelled? If you feel compelled, stop. Compulsion is slavery. Example: Refuse to go along with the crowd.

## How Cosmic Understanding Cures Pressures of Living

Here is a man with a headache. When I ask him how he is curing himself, he replies, "I'm repairing the leak in my roof." I reply, "But how can that cure your headache? You must work on *yourself.*"

So it is with anxiety. Nothing is more pointless than trying to cure our restlessness by involving ourselves in exterior projects. The cure is found in the same place as the problem and that is within the man.

Anxiety exists because we have strayed far from our psychic homeland. Man is like a victim of amnesia who has wandered to a foreign land where everything conflicts with his original position. The strange customs confuse him, his money is worthless, unfamiliar laws keep him tense. Henry David Thoreau describes him as, *The slave and prisoner of his own opinion of himself.* But as he awakens to his true identity, he returns to his homeland and harmony.

The Danish thinker, Soren Kierkegaard, made a profound point about anxiety. He said that it always precedes foolish and self-defeating actions. Therefore, if we can nip apprehension, we can also nip self-defeat.

So pressure springs from false ideas about ourselves and the nature of life on earth. It is profitable to explore false viewpoints.

One false idea is that anyone or anything can hurt you. Events can ruin your reputation, take your money, mistreat you, revenge itself upon you, deceive, betray and abandon you, but cannot hurt you. Try to see that *you* are more valuable than events happening to you, good or bad, just as a peach tree is more valuable than its separate fruits.

We originally picked up our life-damaging attitudes from talkative, but mixed-up, people who did not know they were mixed up. But you and I sense the folly of clinging to mere words from others. We realize that a borrowed feather cannot grow. We see the need for working with what is real within us. And so we ask with Epictetus, *Who in the world, then, is this man who has any authority to make any declaration about you?* We answer, "There is no authority outside the truth itself."

A major cause of anxiety lies in false ideas about goodness. People nervously feel they should be good, but have no idea whatsoever about the nature of true goodness.

## The Way to Contentment with Supermind

As damaging as false notions are, you must never fear them. You must never fear anything at all. You see, false ideas thrive on anxiety. That is how they maintain their tricky hold on the mind. They try to scare you into submission. Refuse. Bravely fight your way out of the net, step by step. Declare with the Sufi mystic, *I will go a thousand leagues in falsehood, that one step of the journey may be true.*

We are not at the mercy of anything that happens to us. We are only at the mercy of our own negative reactions, if we permit it. You need not. No matter how badly other people may treat you, never give your attention to them. Instead, study your own responses to what they said or did, for that is your only problem. Realize that mistreatment exists because the false self labels it as such; thus, you react with all the pains the false self can cause.

You recall in Chapter 12 we discovered that a man consists of hundreds of different selves. Some are beneficial, others destructive. Well, among them, there exists a special self *which takes every event as if it were the very thing you wanted to happen.* That self is the Supermind, which is never upset by anything. Your goal is to nourish it into greater strength. Then, every step is sunlit.

Remember, you cannot judge your freedom from apprehension when things go smoothly. Anyone can feel at ease in a calm sea. It is the stormy crisis that tells the story. How do you react when you lose someone, when defeated or hurt? The purpose of Supermind is to make and keep you strong in both calm and stormy seas.

One way to find contentment is to persistently pass by everything that is *not* contentment. With close observation we may discover that genuine satisfaction is not what we formerly thought it was. We may see that it is not ego-gratification, power, excitement, physical activity nor worldly success. By discarding the counterfeits, we come to the real. It is as if you were searching your garden for a lost diamond ring. You might run across a ring-shaped twig, but you would not accept that as the real thing. You might see a glittering piece of glass, but would know it was not what you wanted. So you keep going until you find the only thing that satisfies — the actual diamond ring.

Too many people are fooled by substitutes. You can easily tell whether you are accepting substitutes or not. Just ask yourself how happy you really are.

Look for the genuine article within the garden of the original self. Somewhere among the mental weeds of false ideas is the diamond we seek. Seek until you find.

Your understanding cures every variety of anxiety, whether over finances, friendships or health. The experimental voyage of Columbus destroyed false theories about a flat earth. Your voyage with the Supermind can leave the false behind and reveal a New World.

Use what might be called the Connecting Technique. Take a single item you wish to conquer. It can be anxiety, a hot temper, shyness, anything at all. Now, connect it with various ideas found in *Supermind*. See, for instance, that shyness is totally unnecessary, that it is part of the false self, that a new kind of boldness can be won and so on.

## The Cause of Daily Pressures

Here is one of the strangest of all anxieties confronting the sincere seeker: He fears that he will succeed in experiencing this or that truth!

Yes, success is frightening. To succeed in attaining the true means we must abandon the false which we cherish because it is familiar, comfortable and because it seems to provide a purpose to life.

We resist what could set us free because we are afraid it will bind us! It is like a prisoner who cringes before an opening door. This peculiar anxiety explains why humanity ignores or persecutes the true teachers. Mankind mistakes their gifts as weapons.

A story from Sufism illustrates this strange situation. A hawk who was owned by a great king lived in the splendor of the palace. One day, while on a flight, he paused to rest in some ruins inhabited by owls. The owls were not wise; they assumed the hawk intended to take over their dreary ruins. The hawk explained his disinterest in their inferior place, mentioning his royal home in the palace. But the owls, knowing nothing of palace life, accused the hawk of using deceitful words in an attempt to rob them.

The cause of daily pressures can be summarized very simply. We meet new challenges with old, unnatural, acquired responses. The solution is obvious. We must abandon habitual responses in favor of simple awareness of the challenge. When met with mental clearness, without the glue of conditioning, there is the challenge but no sticky pressure. This is Supermind-thinking.

Replace *doing* with *seeing*. Never mind if you don't succeed the first thousand times you try. Even when you fail, you succeed, for you are going against the old, useless, mechanical responses.

The Supermind is nothing more nor less than a state of total mental health. In this new state, the mind has gone beyond its usual boundaries of obsessions, superstitions and perplexities. When living from this freshness and wholeness, we live for the first time.

*Man's life begins only with the appearance of rational consciousness* .... (Leo Tolstoy)

## The Natural Life Is True Cosmic Life

I was once in a public building where an official was working hard at acting out his role of public official. He went through all the mechanical motions and facial expressions expected of him. Some children appeared, with all their gaiety and spontaneity. Instantly, the official relaxed and became real, almost a different man than before. He spoke easily and naturally to the children. The children's spontaneity transferred itself to him for just a moment, plainly to his delight and relief.

In this book we have referred to man's original self, his true self, his inner being, all meaning the same. We can explore in a new way by terming it his *natural self*.

A cheery relaxation is man's natural state, just as nature herself is relaxed. A waterfall is concerned only with being itself, not with doing something it considers waterfall-like. It does not force us to think about it; it does not demand our attention and energy; it does not lean on us for gifts; it asks nothing of us. It simply gives what it is, and lets it go at that. And that is why we enjoy its magnificence.

The usual phrase is "Be yourself." We are not following this counsel if we are strained and unsure. These are the sour fruits of the carelessly adopted synthetic self.

Anything we usually classify as mistakes, badness or foolishness can be much more accurately defined as unnaturalness. That is all human error really is — living unnaturally, going against the normal flow of our true nature as demonstrated in the following answers to searching questions:

**Q:** Is there an order in which negativities fall away as we think from the natural Supermind? I mean, will some drop off more easily than others?

**A:** The order varies with each individual, but there is a general rule: The stronger a negativity connects with unnatural ideas one has about himself, the more desperately it clings. This is why pride and vanity stick like glue.

**Q:** Which ones fall away first?

**A:** Early victories are often over petty resentments at being told the truth or over depression when hearing gloomy remarks. Just watch the healthy process in yourself. You can see your loss of unnaturalness as clearly as leaves falling from a tree.

Though there seems to be ten thousand enemies along the path, you have one sure friend, the natural Supermind. It is always trying to break through the wall of artificiality we carelessly build around it. Help this *"imprisoned splendour,"* as Robert Browning called it, to break out.

The mystical teacher J.P. de Caussade states, *All we have to do is to receive what we are given ....* We are given the naturalness to love someone, to be calm in crisis, to ignore self-defeating suggestions, to be pleasant, forgiving, tender, helpful, unworried, brave, energetic.

It helps to realize that you need not *create* any of these natural virtues. You need only *reveal* to yourself what is already created and ready within the Supermind. In the esoteric sense, revelation *is* creation. Grasp this idea and you will feel like a man in the Garden of Eden whose blindfold falls off.

## How to Handle Anxieties

Anxiety arises from a feeling of emptiness. If you will be fully aware of the emptiness, without resistance, and without wishing to escape it, it turns into something new. But have no desire to experience the newness; simply be aware of the emptiness. The magic then happens by itself.

The individual who desperately manufactures artificial activities in order to hide his emptiness from himself is secretly terrified by the question, "But what can I find to do next?" Again, an alert awareness of this condition is a fine start toward destroying both the painful throb and the artificial activities.

It is good news to hear that consciousness has power to destroy pressures of which we are unaware. They are able to bother us only because we are unconscious of their existence. The vast majority of pressures are like sea mines below the surface of the water, which blow up unwary ships. One unseen anxiety is the idea of being cheated out of the good fortune enjoyed by others. We look enviously at the man with a higher salary or longer vacation, and feel cheated. Awareness frees us from that form of self-torture.

Let me give you a surprising and quite revealing experiment. The next time someone tells you how anxious or worried he is, reply, "The situation may be exactly as you describe it, but tell me why should you be anxious over it?" I guarantee that if he really hears your question, it will startle him. He may answer you, but in no case will it be a calm, accurate or realistic answer. His reply will be emotional and he may sputter, frown or sigh.

His answer will not be realistic because, in reality, there *is* no reason why he should be anxious. There just isn't, even if he doesn't see it. That is why he must give you a non-realistic reply, based on his confused emotions and false ideas about life.

This is the exact lesson taught by Jesus, Lao-tse, Socrates and every other advanced teacher: *Be anxious over nothing.* Take this as if it means exactly what it says: "Be anxious over nothing."

## The Cure for Fear

So many people have asked for help in curing their fears that I am going to set out their questions and my answers for your guidance.

**Q:** Your books have helped me realize something for the very first time. I am aware of how frightened I actually am. Could we please discuss the cause and cure of fear?

**A:** I will explain the entire problem in as simple a way as possible. You can then make a persistent effort to penetrate its full meaning. A man lives in a sand castle made up of imaginary ideas about himself, false moralities and neurotic demands. He has false notions about everything, including human relations, worldly success, religion. Now, he is afraid that someone or something will come along and destroy this false structure. So he resists whatever threatens him, thus making him not only fearful, but also suspicious and hostile.

**Q:** You mean he fears the destruction of his own falseness?

**A:** Yes. He mistakenly takes this false identity as *himself*. He assumes that his identity is made up of this bundle of imaginary ideas, which it is not. But since he thinks so, he will fight fiercely anything threatening to destroy it. He actually believes he is saving himself, when in fact he is perpetuating his own misery. His false sense of self must go before his true identity can come.

**Q:** And how can he surrender his falseness?

**A:** This can be done by permitting the sand castle to collapse and by not resisting the waves of reality. Then, having no false structure to protect, he is no longer afraid. We are afraid only when defending artificiality, when hiding something.

**Q:** Please supply an example.

**A:** You want a certain event to occur. It fails to come, which makes you anxious. Perhaps your usual reaction is to feel resentful or to blame someone. But you now wish to understand, so you look inward. You discover that you wanted the event because you assumed it would provide excitement or security. You realize the falseness of this, because no external event can do anything for you. So you surrender your need for this false sense of security. The moment you do, fear ceases.

**Q:** As you suggest, I will work at understanding all this.

**A:** Good. You will then see that there is no need to be scared about anything whatsoever.

There is an *attitude* you can adopt which insures steady advancement toward newness. Before presenting it, I want to assure you of its deep significance, far deeper than words can convey. We have seen that the inner state of most people can be described in one word: *"frozen."* But you no longer want the pain arising from a frozen mind, you want the flowing freedom of the river.

*Cease to blame anyone for anything and you will find release and relief.* No matter what happens to you, do not look for someone or something to blame. Blaming others cuts off healing insight. Not blaming increases self-responsibility and self-success. Most accusations toward others are subconscious; we do not see them. But as mystic Meister Eckhart pointed out, *A stone beneath the surface of the ground is just as heavy as a visible one.* To be rid of the load, blame nothing, but seek to understand why things happen as they do.

## How to Live to Please Yourself

A man would be shocked to see how little he lives to please *himself*. This is the great problem. He fails to see that his day is spent in unconscious slavery to pain, in serving false desires which he takes as necessities, in doubts and unwanted habits. So close are these negativities to him that he cannot conceive of any other state. So he submits to his chains with a combination of despair and secret rebellion.

But the shock of seeing this can also be a happy revelation. Awareness of the way we are can change the way we are. The man who lives from his Supermind truly lives to please himself. Depending upon nothing but his own Kingdom of Heaven within, you have nothing to give him, nor can you take anything away. He is indifferent to both praise and criticism.

He lives to please himself, but it is not, as some might think, a selfish state. It is the exact opposite; it is the only genuine generosity. The self-pleasing man, the liberated man, offers a supreme gift to others — an invitation to experience new life.

You don't need to think of yourself as a spiritual seeker. It is a back-bending burden to go around with a self-picture of being a spiritual or religious person. A man is genuinely spiritual when he has no conditioned ideas of what it means to be spiritual. To be real is to be spiritual. A cat is normal because no one has fixed him with the neurotic notion that he should be a tiger. A man loses neurosis when he is what he is.

India's advanced teacher, Sri Ramakrishna, told the story of some men who wandered around a mango grove, examining the branches and leaves. But another man was much wiser. He ate the mangoes. That is what we must do. We must not waste ourselves with pointless theologies or by endlessly talking about esoteric matters. We must consume the very fruit.

Remember this encouraging psychic law: *To the same degree that a Cosmic Truth frightens us, to that same degree can it heal.* If we bravely face the fact, without evading or resisting it, that very fact can make us whole. For instance, suppose our self-observation reveals jealousy within us. This may be so unpleasant that we want to turn away and deny it. But if we simply face the jealousy and see it as an acquired habit, not as part of the essential self, we weaken its hold on us.

Self-awareness is the magic light which banishes darkness.

To make progress does not mean that you necessarily take a jolt from life with surface calmness. In almost every case, those people who appear to be calm in a crisis are severely shocked within and have only an appearance of quietness. We make progress by seeing how distressed we really are and by letting life jolt us in any way it likes, but without putting the feeling of "I" into the jolt. *You* cannot be jolted; only the conditioned "I" is hurt.

To live rightly, you must first live fully. You must courageously expose yourself to every event and person without knowing or caring what happens to your present beliefs. Defensiveness prevents full experiencing, which could free you. An individual who thinks his defensiveness is a castle is really in prison. His castle is found at last when he dares to venture forth to meet and slay the dragons.

If you timidly avoid a friend with whom you quarreled, you remain afraid. If you permit a meeting with that friend, *with no preconceived ideas of what to say or do,* you destroy fear.

## How Your New Life of Pleasing Yourself Begins

Living to please ourselves does not mean to gratify every desire that comes along. This is a challenging idea to grasp at first, because we fear doing without the gratification. We wrongly think it benefits us. So powerful is this illusion that we persist in harmful desires, even while they destroy us!

Let's take the common desire to have others behave in a way that gratifies; for example, we want them to respect us. When they don't, we get upset. Why? It is not because of their disrespect, but because of our desire-demand that they appreciate us. If we let them behave any way they like, we are free. We are no longer slaves to our own desire.

As long as *you* are all right, what does it matter how others treat you? It matters not at all. Is the flight of a bird through the woods disturbed by shadows?

Let's re-examine the enemy of the free life — a false sense of self.

A man does not live from his authentic nature. He lives from dozens of dream-pictures about himself. The dream-pictures, which he takes as real, dominate his feelings and command his behavior, all to his deterioration. A businessman has the idea of being important to his community. When not asked to play a role in a community project, he feels mistreated, only because he thinks he needs to be important. If he didn't care whether he was important or not, he would shrug his shoulders over the supposed mistreatment. This small example represents the great illusion responsible for every problem and anguish on earth. It is an ego-centered illusion that man has a separate identity, that he is something apart from the Cosmic Whole. It breeds pressure, resentment, treachery against others. Man's false belief in a separate identity resembles an island which is apparently cut off from the mainland, though they are actually one and the same beneath the surface.

Suppose you visited a motion picture studio. You walk down the set made up of a row of homes. So far so good. But what happens if you enter a front door and try to make yourself comfortable? Discomfort. Ease is impossible because the scene is make-believe.

That is exactly what happens to us. Not realizing that we live in false fronts, we try to settle down and are shocked.

*We must begin to suspect that we are not who we think we are. We must wake up.*

As long as a man fears to extinguish his false sense of self, he must pay its price of hounding pressures. But with his willingness to let go of everything false about himself, he begins the new life of comfort.

You need not frantically battle the false self, like you might battle against a locked door. It is to be seen through, for the door is glass.

## The Art of Practical Selfishness with Supermind

You will be amazed at how the daily pressures of life fade away when you learn to think from your Supermind. Maybe you presently find yourself making promises to others which you later regret. This is a constant source of irritation to you, probably unconscious. You are torn between two choices. Should you keep your promise, while resenting it, or should you cancel out while feeling guilty?

But now you are becoming a psychic artist. You are doing things differently. You no longer make promises to others because you want them to like you or because it seems the easy way out of an awkward situation. No. You no longer place their approval before your inner sense of what is right for you. You dare to call your time and energy your own. And so, self-division and self-pressure fade.

Every day you must decide which you want most — your integrity or the approval of others. Then, you must place your integrity first. It calls for courage. Why? Because when you stop pleasing people in order to live your own life, they will resent not being able to use you any more. They may even accuse you of selfishness. Never mind. As they angrily depart, give a cheer for what you have done for yourself.

## For a Life of Natural Ease

1. We can learn to work rightly for ourselves with Supermind.

2. Pressure springs from false and conditioned ideas about life.

3. You are not at the mercy of anything that merely "happens."

4. Permit your Supermind to reveal its full power for your serenity.

5. Do not resist the very cosmic force that can free you from distresses.

6. The Supermind is a state of total mental health.

7. You need not create goodness, only reveal it and it will take over for you.

8. There is no reason whatsoever for your fear and anxiety.

9. You can learn to live to please yourself properly.

# 14

## How to Have Total Freedom Through the Supermind

Suppose you and a friend are forced to land your airplane in an isolated wilderness. As you wander around, your friend stubs his toe on a rock. You are astonished to hear him remark, "There are too many rocks in this place. We had better make plans to reduce them to pebbles."

A few moments later you are drenched by a slashing rain, which brings another surprising comment from your friend, "Terrible rainfall in this place. Let's get busy to control it."

Next, both of you are chased by wild beasts. After escaping, your friend speaks out, "There is another reform we must make in this place. We must train the wild animals to behave decently." Sadly shaking his head, he adds, "There's a lot of wrong things for us in this place."

You would tell him, "Of course everything is all wrong. *We are in the wrong place.* There's no point trying to change its conditions; our task is to alter our relationship to it. We must work our way back to freedom. Then, everything will be all right."

So it is with us. There is no use fighting the place. We are much more intelligent than that. We can see that we are in the wrong place mentally. We can change our psychological relationship with the world of people and events. We can cease being victimized by the rocks and rains of savage humanity. We can do this by marching out of the wilderness to our own freedom.

In her poem, *The Prisoner*, Emily Brontë speaks of her mystical experience:

*Then dawns the Invisible: the Unseen its truth reveals;*

*My outward sense is gone, my inward essence feels;*

*Its wings are almost free — its home, its harbour found.*

*Measuring the gulf, it stoops, and dares the final bound.*

## What Freedom Should Mean to You

Except for the word *"love,"* I doubt if any word is more loosely used and less understood than *"freedom."*

Spiritually speaking, there is no such thing as financial, political or geographical freedom. You can be a millionaire, live in a land of liberty, have your home in a quiet countryside and still be imprisoned by your own negativities. There is only one freedom — self-freedom. All else is masquerade. I have seen much of this. I have given talks in luxurious homes occupied by people living in mental dungeons.

A vital point must be made. It is not enough to give lip service to this. Everyone quickly agrees that inner wealth is all that counts. But spoken agreement means nothing if it is contradicted by unconscious desire for wealth. It is like saying *yes*, while shaking the head *no*. We must be in conscious agreement, based on inner understanding of true value, for that is what changes us. That is what makes our daily behavior entirely different. It has been said, "The man who can find pearls will not stop to collect shells."

Just as a cloud blocks our view of the sun, so does wrong thinking cut us off from reality. By working at the removal of thought-clouds, we view the brightness beyond. Mental clarity is freedom itself. That is why you need never do anything, in the usual sense of doing, to free yourself. To try to find freedom in mere activity won't work. We must try to understand non-freedom. That is what works. You really don't want to *do*. You want to *be*.

Therefore, what do we mean by not being free? We mean it in very practical ways in both the Inner World and the Outer World. Non-freedom is the inability to break off a painful mental movie, to be nervous while at the end of a long line at the market, to have a critical spirit, to resentfully feel that one gives more than one gets, to chase after people in frantic hope they can do one some good. Can a person living like this think he is free?

Non-freedom is when a man is split in many contradictory parts. One part of him wants to buy a new car, but another part refuses to cooperate. One desire drives him to a place of amusement, but another desire is unamused.

Freedom is internal harmony, where thoughts, emotions and physical movements all cheerfully do the same thing. They are in agreement, having no argument with each other. It is like the harmony produced by the separate strings of a guitar when plucked by a skilled musician.

Everything within you reacts harmoniously when you learn the principles of psychic music with Supermind.

## A Startling Revelation of Self-Knowledge in Supermind

Note how one of my students found the light of Supermind in the following exchange of thoughts:

**Q:** I would like freedom from painful thoughts.

**A:** You may feel that you are compelled to submit to painful thoughts, but you are not. They are without genuine power. With psychic awakening, you can stand aside and watch them pass by, just as you stand on a riverbank and watch a raging river, while being personally untouched.

**Q:** I am willing to follow inner guidance, but don't know what it is. How can I recognize authentic intuition?

**A:** You can recognize such by first detecting its counterfeit which appears as fanciful imaginations or hounding desires. Be watchful. Counterfeits bring grief. The true inner voice leaves you with a sense of health and sanity.

**Q:** Now that I am working on myself with the principles of the Supermind, I seem to have more conflicts than before!

**A:** No, you are merely aware of the internal conflicts that you have been unconsciously enduring for years. This in itself is progress. To tame the lion you must enter his cage.

One thing is certain: We cannot find our freedom until we first see our imprisonment. What really bothers us is what we hide from ourselves. We refuse to look down into our cluttered cellars. To complicate it even more, we will not even admit the concealment of anything. There is a way to break this self-defeating habit.

Come to sudden stops throughout your day to become aware of heavy, grinding feelings within yourself. Be strict with yourself. You will observe that you are not as at ease as you imagined. Remember, it is not negative to see negativity within yourself. It is refreshingly positive self-knowledge.

A strange revelation comes when you look within. At the same time that you see negative features, you also observe positive powers. Both are within, so your awareness of old weakness is followed by consciousness of new strength. But weakness must be noticed *first*. If it does not occur in this order, the strength will be counterfeit and will desert you.

I want to show you another way to make self-watchfulness work for your benefit. Some day, while anxiously doing something you consider vital and necessary, catch yourself long enough to inquire, "Why am I doing this?" You may discover that the seemingly important task is really trivial and wasteful. You now know something valuable you never knew before.

## Words and Their Meaning for Self-Liberty

Humans orate about love without being loving, chatter about charity while lacking it themselves, discuss heavenly topics while thinking about earthly profits. This wilderness of words is explained by George Fox, founder of the Society of Friends, as follows: *They did not possess what they professed.*

This introduces word-worshipping, a trap which the freedom-seeker must avoid. The use of high-sounding and idealistic words is a subtle trick of the false self, presenting counterfeits for realities. The word-worshipper is enslaved by his own contradictions because of unawareness, like the man who declared, "I may not always be right, but I am never wrong."

We are going far beyond word-juggling to basic mental wholeness, to truthfulness, to cosmic consciousness. We want and need nothing else. *All beside love is but words.* (Abbas Effendi)

First we must realize the inadequacy of language when trying to explain inner activities. How would we define the terms *consciousness* and *awareness*, used often in this book? Well, we can say they are mental states where we see things as they really are. But that in turn requires explanation. The fact is that mental states must be experienced to be individually known. Words have limited, though definite, use as bridges on the road to understanding. *The best is not to be explained by words.* (Leo Tolstoy)

Watch your own reactions to words. Certain words arouse strong emotional feelings, such as *sex, money, God, love, hatred.* Try to see that you are responding to mere labels, to your acquired ideas about things and not to the things themselves. In order to act clearly, we must drop our associative thinking built up from the past.

Suppose some hikers come to a road sign pointing them in the direction they want to go. But instead of hiking ahead, they argue over the sign itself. One says it should be a foot taller, another wished it had some pretty ornaments. We cannot advance toward the Supermind if we pause to chatter about the road signs. Words are words and cannot be anything else. For a man to talk frequently about God does not make him godly, any more than talking about the sun makes him a sunbeam. This is what Meister Eckhart had in mind with his famous line, *If you would be perfect, don't chatter about God.*

Do not try to define life. If you call it absurd, you are saying it should be sensible according to your exclusive viewpoints. If you insist it is meaningful, you will soon change your mind when unexpected events upset your comfortable position. Stop philosophizing. Leave life alone. It neither needs nor heeds our wordy definitions.

Live according to Cosmic Truth of Supermind. That is all you need to do. Why look for anything else to do? In that free state, your day is neither absurd nor meaningful; it is simply what it is. This is an entirely new kind of inspiration, unfettered with fears, frustrations and all the other negatives humans are prone to cling to.

## Achieving Freedom from Fear

Suppose you see a stage hypnotist make a man think he is being chased by a wolf. The man races around fearfully. To help that man, you would not tell him to run faster or to strike at the wolf with a club. You would try to wake him up.

That is what we must do — wake up to things as they are. *Fear must be entirely banished. The purified soul will fear nothing.* (Plotinus)

Don't *try* to be unafraid. That is impossible. Rather, go ahead while being afraid. That is the entire secret for abolishing fear.

The Supermind teaches us to have no self-concern at all. Whatever happens to you, act as though it happened to someone else. A person once asked me, "You say that the present moment is free from fear, that peace exists right now. If this is so, how come I'm anxious right now?"

I answered, "Because you do not realize the freedom of right now. Quite unconsciously you think with memories of past pains, thus covering the present with a veil of remembrances. Try to see that nothing exists except right now. Start by noticing the connection between your fear and the memory of a frightening event of the past."

Perhaps a man fears confusion. Watch how he reacts to it. Notice how eagerly he seeks to relieve his pressure. Watch how quickly he speaks up or argues when the confusion involves disagreement with another person. He cannot find an answer like this. It merely calls into play the *conditioned mind* with all its defensive opinions. It is like calling up an army of aggressive soldiers to establish a peace group; they know nothing of the subject.

A new self-awareness is needed. It appears when the man is quiet, not fighting the confusion. Answers to life's perplexities cannot be found with a fixed mind. They come *effortlessly when the conditioned mind is still.*

I will tell you of a terror that tyrannizes millions of people. Since it is always an unconscious terror, people do not see what it does to them. As you study this idea, try to see whether it applies to you.

It is the fear of *nothing happening.*

Look at it. Have you noticed the arising of a vague uneasiness when there is nothing to occupy the mind, when nothing happens and nothing seems likely to occur?

Upon feeling this emptiness, a man does something — anything — to escape its pain. But that is only a distraction. Sooner or later, the party is over and the same dread reenters the front door.

Seeking escape is not the answer. *Not* escaping is the answer.

## How to Cease All Anxious Effort

Can you sit quietly and examine the fright of nothing happening? Can you try to not run away from it? As a matter of fact, you cannot run away any more than you can escape your body by running with your legs. No, you cannot *escape*, but you can *understand*, which is quite another thing.

Throw your so-called securities to the winds. Do you dare to do it? Expose yourself to losing everything upon which you depend, including exterior happenings. Drop the whole anxious mess. Do nothing, have nothing, be nothing. Stop planning to keep yourself safe. Can you even give up caring whether you are safe or not? If so, you are getting close.

*To a mind that is still, the whole universe surrenders.* (Chuang-tse)

With new resolution declare, "I do not know the answer to this. I simply realize that I do not know and am willing to let it go at that. I do not seek an answer through my habitual thinking. I choose to be without an answer. I stop. I just stop. That's all there is to it."

When you seek no answer, it will be there, with Supermind.

You have no responsibility for *making* your life roll forward. You have every responsibility for *letting* it roll. Cease all effort to make your life move. See that life moves all by itself. I demonstrated this freedom in answering questions below after one of my lectures:

**Q:** You seem to imply that everything we do is an escape from facing ourselves. What about taking a vacation? Is that an escape?

**A:** It can be an escape or it can be fun. If you unconsciously use it as an escape, you won't have nearly the fun than if you didn't. If you don't care whether you take a vacation or not, you are on vacation every day of the year.

**Q:** I am a slave to rush and tension. How can I slow down?

**A:** You are enslaved because you falsely think you have somewhere to go, psychologically speaking. Have you noticed that you cannot define your destination; you just rush around? You have no place to go. You are already there, but don't see it. It is as if you walk the Paris streets while yearning to be in France. Try to see that you are already where you want to be, then rush falls away.

**Q:** Please let me speak frankly. I fear my lust and greed.

**A:** Do not be afraid of yourself. There is nothing in you that psychic awakening cannot cure. You have merely identified yourself with lust and greed. You are afraid because you mistakenly take them as part of yourself. Work at seeing them as entirely apart from your true nature. Self-fright then vanishes.

## How to Find Lasting Delight

The march toward inner freedom is like a man who must cross a series of rivers in order to reach home. The rivers have various names such as Stubbornness, Imitation, Unnaturalness, Timidity. If he refuses to enter the water and wade through, he remains fixed where he is, cut off from the comforts of home. But by daring the conflict, he passes beyond himself, getting closer and closer to his heart's desire.

When we have passed beyond the painful cravings connected with food and sex, we have come a long way. The liberated man does not and need not tell himself what he needs. He leaves his needs to Life itself, which always knows what it is doing. He does not interfere by reaching out to grab. He waits until life offers and then receives. He is hounded by neither food nor sex; they are below him as servants, not above him as dictators.

Plotinus explains it with the following words:

*What desire there may be can never be for the vile; even the food and drink necessary for restoration will lie outside the soul's attention, and not less the sexual appetite ... it will turn upon the actual needs of the nature and be entirely under control.*

We have seen the need for rising above human definitions of success. Therefore, what is the *Supermind* meaning of success? A relaxed and friendly effort to understand esoteric facts is success. Forget the results of your efforts, for they arrive all by themselves. The effort alone is all that counts. *Genuine effort is success.*

The techniques leading to celestial success are not complicated. The only complication is man's reluctance to patiently practice. For instance, will we recognize self-defeating behavior in ourselves and then refuse to defend it? That technique alone works wonders, for nothing on earth is more healthy or refreshing than honesty.

Man lives heavily because he refuses to release his acquired negativity, like a sea gull unable to fly because it insistently clings to a heavy fish.

But Meister Eckhart encourages, *A free mind has power to achieve all things.*

How does it work in practical situations? Here is a superb system for making unpleasant work easy and carefree. Do it with your mind, not with your emotions. Any kind of work, whether housework, office duties, business affairs, should be done with the mind, never with the feelings. By refusing to let your emotions take over, you cannot possibly resent or dislike what you are doing. Try it. Use your reasoning mind only. Work ceases to be work!

It is a genuine and lasting delight to understand and experience a truth that sets you free.

## How to Be Free of Domination from Others

The following excerpt from one of my question and answer periods after a lecture illustrates how to be free of negative domination:

**Q:** Please explain what you mean by freedom from others.

**A:** It is quite simple. You are chained to anyone from whom you want something, whom you depend upon for self-satisfaction. You are free from anyone from whom you want nothing. A Supermind principle is that no other person can give you authentic enrichment; it must come from within yourself. When this is clearly understood, your human relations are right.

**Q:** I weakly submit myself to people who seem stronger than I, which I don't like. I'm especially afraid of angry people.

**A:** An angry man is not strong; he is weak. Never give an unawakened man an opportunity to explode his anger or sarcasm onto you. You fall into his trap whenever you appear weak or whenever he senses that you want something from him. The animal-nature in human beings is always on the lookout for someone to attack. Refuse to be a target.

**Q:** A certain person never stops bad behavior toward me.

**A:** If someone continually behaves badly toward you, it is because you are, in some unconscious way, rewarding his bad action. You reward it because of a false need within yourself. Try to see this false need. When it falls away, you will withdraw your reward, which produces a crisis. The other person will criticize and perhaps leave you. This means you must have courage to stand alone. Eventually, you will see the necessity of the crisis to your freedom.

If someone rejects you, your inner understanding of the situation can keep you free. But if you reject another, you are psychologically chained to him. We reject another whenever we feel him to be a threat to our imaginary sense of self. But when this spurious self is extinguished, no one is a threat. In this state you can come and go among people as you please, immune from hurt, no matter how they treat you.

One freedom enjoyed by the enlightened person is that of living by his own rules. His conduct arises from his Supermind, which is truly moral, authentically decent, genuinely compassionate. He does what he pleases, which cannot be said of anyone enslaved by the compulsions of unnatural desires. The captive mind pleases imaginary ideas about its own greatness, receiving imaginary rewards.

Also, when living from the natural laws of your own being, you are free from the pressures of any foolish man-made laws, of which there are plenty. The free man is his own law. But, it is not the fake independence characterized by public rebellion and arrogance. It is quiet, unseen, truly humble. When a man knows spiritual secrets without needing to talk about them, he really knows.

## How to Have No Concern for Yourself

You are free when you have no anxious thoughts about what happens to you. You are quietly carried along by daily events with no personal concern as to their effect upon you. Nothing bothers you. It is a state of neither liking nor disliking, resisting nor accepting, but only of flowing along.

Do not think this idea fantastic. Do not think it will make life dull. It is nothing like that at all. It is the more abundant life. Explore with me.

A man possessing the secrets of Supermind, perhaps someone like the Dutch mystic Baruch Spinoza, would point out, "The more you struggle to live, the less you live. Give up the notion that you must be sure of what you are doing. Instead, surrender to what is real within you, for that alone is sure. As stars are high above earth, you are above everything distressing. But you must awaken to it. Wake up!"

The final decision as to what is good or bad for you, as to what is right or wrong, cannot be made by a conditioned mind. The habitual mind cannot find anything but its own confusion. It always decides on the basis of excitement, of ego-gratification, which means that all its choices are wrong. If unawake, we cannot and we need not decide what is good because *we do not really know*. Therefore, we need only get out of our own way, leaving final decisions to the Supermind, which is always right.

Try to see that *you* don't decide anything. What makes a decision is the dominant desire of the moment, which is not the total *you*. This explains the frequent confession, "One minute I want *this*, and the next minute *that*."

What a happy life when *you do not need to know what to do with yourself!* Reflect on this.

When confronted by life's challenges, there are two ways of saying, "I don't know what to do." One way is useless, the other is peaceful. The useless way is when you say, "I don't know what to do" because you are caught between two or more opposing desires. What you really mean is, "I can't decide between several choices." But when the free man says, "I don't know what to do," there is no pain or conflict because there are no opposing desires. He need not know what to do because there is nothing to know. He is already at peace. Not knowing is no problem to him because he sees that whatever happens, all is well.

We clear our minds of confusion not by settling upon this or that drifting raft of desire, but by swimming beyond all acquired desires. We then reach that wonderful shore hinted at by esoteric teachers: "When you know nothing, you know everything." So press on, from one victory to the next. If, in your quest, you dare the discomfort, you will find on that new shore a kind of comfort unknown by those who do not dare.

So, whenever you meet a spiritual or psychological truth, do not try to interpret it. Just observe it without comment, just as you would silently observe a new kind of flower. Do not inform a truth what it should be according to your judgment; let it inform you what it is, all by itself. Truth is found in the silent self.

Awareness can be developed to where confusion can be snapped off like a light bulb. Since confusion is merely an offspring of psychic sleep, freedom comes by snapping out of it.

## How Your Deliverance Dawns

We must see liberation as a *return*. We must return to the unlimited self, the non-mechanical self.

Non-free behavior is always done in mechanical unawareness. And mechanical unawareness indicates unhappiness. At one time I stopped into a shop to ask for a certain article. While I was still telling the saleswoman what I wanted, her head began to shake to indicate the product was not in stock. She said *no* even before she knew what I wanted. When she finally heard me out, she gestured toward the desired article.

Let's study this incident. Why would she shake her head before hearing the facts? Perhaps because her deeply ingrained negative nature mechanically extended itself to an exterior situation, producing a mistake. That incident reveals a thousand things about her inner situation. She is unhappy, for mechanical negativity is always unhappy. She does not think; she merely responds according to acquired habits. And so on.

Deliverance dawns when you:

> *Prefer the true to the exciting*
>
> *Pause before you react*
>
> *Shed the influence of the last person you met*
>
> *Permit the self to teach the self*
>
> *Practice self-honesty to where it hurts*

*Shun sentimental dramatics posing as reality*
*No longer look for relief outside yourself*
*See that the penalty for falseness is immediate*
*See through public pretensions of piety*
*Make a truth your very own truth*

It is wise procedure to specify a particular area where you wish to be free. Select an area where you are obviously unfree. Could it be a hounding need for approval, feelings of guilt or an obsession? Perhaps it is your inability to cease pursuit of fulfillments that never fulfill.

Select a single area and pour over it for every ounce of knowledge and wisdom obtainable.

You will find that release from one area provides freedom from others, just as the lopping of a large branch destroys those connected to it.

Here is how to strike a blow for personal liberty: Whenever in a crisis of any kind, recall an appropriate principle of the *Supermind*. It helps ten times more than reflections made when things are smooth. Psychic hypnosis is snapped when you deliberately tear your mind away from the crisis to the principle. If a crisis makes you feel angry or guilty toward yourself, remember that you are neither your own goodness nor badness. When this is actually perceived, you live on the mountaintop.

*Step out of your cave; the world waits for you as a garden.* (Nietzsche) You have a secret self, a free and a whole self, which lives in a garden. It grieves over nothing and asks favors of no one. It knows what it is doing. It rests in its own serenity. That secret self is your Supermind.

## Special Truths About Freedom

1. Freedom is a state of mental clarity as to your Supermind powers.

2. It is a positive act to control our negativities.

3. Go beyond mere words to the experience of cosmic freedom.

4. When the conditioned mind is still, true liberty appears.

5. Abandon all nervous concern for yourself; take no thought for the evils of tomorrow.

6. Cosmic awakening is the sure cure for all ills, mental and physical.

7. All your sincere effort toward freedom with Supermind is a success.

8. Happiness is found in freedom from the false and conditioned self.

9. Work consistently with the principles of the Supermind and you will always succeed.

# 15

## How to Have Everything Right Through the Supermind

How can a man start to live in a way that makes everything right at last? Very simple. He must clearly see that he is not presently living as he really wants. In this book I have shown how Supermind can change and benefit your life. The chapters containing the principles of Supermind can be used by you as stepping stones in developing your understanding. Here in the remaining few pages I shall highlight the main points.

In my previous writing, *The Mystic Path to Cosmic Power*, I reviewed the classic story told by Plato, the tale of the prisoners in the cave. In summary, a group of men in a cave were under the illusion that they were free. Prisoners of their own false beliefs, they assumed that their dark and miserable world was the only world there was. They were so chained by their ignorance that they scorned anyone who came down to tell them of the bright and free world outside.

Their delusion is mankind's delusion. Men insist they are free, but are not .... *They everywhere teem with so many forms of folly and daily devise so many new ones ....* (Erasmus) But it is extremely difficult to get men to see this.

A chief obstacle to awakening is explained by an Eastern proverb, *You cannot speak to a summer insect about ice.* An imprisoned man cannot compare his confinement with liberty because he has no liberty with which to compare it. It is like trying to compare a tree in your yard with a tree growing in a remote canyon in New Zealand.

This is why that first glimpse of something entirely different is necessary. A man can follow it all the way to newness, just as Columbus nearing the New World followed a flight of birds to the island of San Salvador.

Our first responsibility in life is toward our own inner awakening. Unless this is done, we are working in the wrong order. Half the world's grief is caused by irresponsible egotists who think they have a divine mission to be responsible for others. Only self-responsibility can develop that center from which genuine aid can radiate. Besides, there cannot be personal peace without personal responsibility.

## How to Live the Effortless Life

It cannot be emphasized enough that insight into things as they really are in Supermind brings an enormous relief from pressures. One such relief comes when you see that you are not your own badness any more than you are your own goodness. Guilt goes forever. It is a painful and egotistical mistake to think of ourselves as being wicked or abnormal. We are neither our own goodness nor badness. This relieving insight comes after a certain point in self-development for Supermind.

Here is how to be relaxed and effortless in your relations with people: Never contrive to make a relationship either a close or a distant one. Do not permit your desires or ambitions to interfere with the natural flow of events. Let the relationship fall into its own place spontaneously, for in that is enjoyment. It is not your duty to determine the closeness of a relationship. Your only duty is to be a real person in it.

## How to Have Everything Right Through the Supermind

François Fénelon summarizes the effortless life: *Be free, gay, uncomplicated, a child. But be a strong child, fearing nothing* ....

The discovery of wrong procedure must come before the revelation of right procedure. The right is an absence of the wrong, just as a clear sky is the absence of clouds. Our encounter with the wrong way is quite obvious — it hurts! In one way or another, we don't like it. The wrong way is like a stupid enemy who insists upon telling you how to defeat him. If we suffer, that very suffering is telling us that we are wrong about something. Acting intelligently upon that information, we can work toward rightness.

Take the lesson from Taoism about rolling with life. You can easily tell when you are pushing life, rather than rolling with it, by the resulting strain and anxiety. Strain stops when pushing stops.

You want to accomplish something in the Outer World. You push hard. The project fails and you feel bad. The project failed because you picked out a certain rock, called it yours and tried to push it downhill. But you can't push this or that rock. It either rolls downhill by itself or not at all.

You cannot push a rock that attracts you, but you can follow downhill whatever rock happens to roll. There is no strain or anxiety in this. If it should stop anywhere along the way, do not try to push it further and do not be upset or angry. It is not up to you whether it rolls in the first place or whether it stops or not along the way. Look around. There are other rocks you can follow if you wish. Enjoy their easy roll, but do not call them your own. No person can take them from you, but Reality can, but that is always for good, not harm.

Push no rock. Follow the rolling rock. You are wisely harmonizing with life the Supermind way.

## Welcome New Experiences with Supermind

We have covered many things that a man in his heart of hearts does not really want, like pointless activities and noisy involvements. What, then, does he truly aspire to win?

*Self-knowledge*

*Self-unity*

*Self-delight*

*Self-command*

*Self-awareness*

*Self-confidence*

*Self-peace*

They come with ease as we welcome the great transformation brought about by the Supermind.

Try this welcoming exercise: Go through a single day without trying to force things to happen the way you wish. Just go about your business, while letting everything happen the way it wants to happen. Refrain from trying to influence anyone or anything to turn in the direction you desire. Desire nothing. Be content. Do not be a doer, but a quiet follower of all that happens.

Try the above experimentally for a single day. Something entirely different will stir within you. You will suspect something. That something is a higher force — a Reality of Cosmic Truth. By making your desiring-self passive, you give it an opportunity to operate to enrich you.

We must learn to say *yes* to life, with no concern as to what the affirmation brings our way. We need neither know nor care, for it is good, even when we do not know it.

## The Secret of Secrets

Suppose you are in the home of friends, where their young daughter gives her first piano recital. She plays well, but because she is still a student, she strikes a wrong note or two and her timing is imperfect. As she concludes, you applaud in appreciation. There is not the slightest criticism of her mistakes. Do you know what you really applaud? It is her *honest effort*. She did what she *could* do. It arouses genuine tenderness to see this sincere young lady who did her best to play well.

Now, this is the same attitude we must have toward our own faltering steps toward wholeness. We must not condemn or criticize when we strike a wrong note, as will happen frequently. Our sincere intention to do the best we can for the present is all that matters.

I don't know anything more delightfully refreshing than to observe an honest effort toward self-betterment.

So have no worry if you do not know what it means to be receptive or to work earnestly toward the Supermind. If you have no idea whatsoever as to what you are doing, be at ease. Your first task is not to know, but to see clearly that you do not know. This is something you can do at this very moment.

Surrender to the fact that you do not know and leave it right there, for that is an act of healthy receptivity. This kind of surrender is victory.

You constantly ask yourself, "What am I going to do about this?" The reason this bewilderment repeats itself month after month, year after year, is because you do the wrong thing with it. You answer it with a prison-conditioned mind, which always has an answer and always the wrong one.

Now, there is a totally new way of responding to your question, "What am I going to do about this?" It is the way of the Supermind.

Just go ahead with your usual affairs with the realization

that, for the present, you do not know what to do. You see, it is not what you do that counts anyway. It is what you deeply *understand*. Try to grasp this.

Here we have a fine opportunity for setting aside any prides and pretenses we observe within us, for they are obstacles to the new answer. Whoever prefers his pride to truth will not be able to crash through. But you and I want to pass beyond the painful pressure of pride, so we cheerfully set it aside.

The secret of secrets? Here it is:

*Surrender to the fact that you do not know, and leave it right there, for that is an act of healthy receptivity.*

## How to Build Your New World

*A happy life consists in a mind which is free, upright, undaunted and steadfast, beyond the influence of fear or desire.* (Seneca)

Take this as if it means exactly what it says. Do not dilute it by a present inability to grasp it totally. Stand on it solidly. The meaning behind these words are perfectly capable of supporting *you* at this very moment. The following answers to my students' questions illustrate the meaning:

**Q:** Of all the teachings about the Supermind, the most baffling is when you say we should not live in hope. Why, if I had no hope for something better, I couldn't bear it.

**A:** There is true hope and false hope. Suppose you plan to meet someone whom you desperately hope can do you some good. You meet him or her with high hope, only to have it dashed. You are now hurt because you hoped this person would fulfill you.

**Q:** Yet this is the way everyone lives. How awful. But what is the alternative?

**A:** Meet every person and circumstance with no preconceived hopes whatsoever. You see, it is the shattered hope that hurts, not the outcome itself. Live without false hope and you will know the victory of true hope.

**Q:** True hope?

**A:** It arises with your intuitive insight that you are making everything right at last.

If your world falls apart under conditioned thinking, good for you. It wasn't much of a world anyway, was it? Now, by using your basic intelligence with Supermind, you can build a new world. But you must be sure you do not merely prop up the ruins of your old world, while mistaking it for newness. Newness is not a rebuilding of the old; it is starting with absolutely nothing, and permitting the new to build itself with its own materials. You can be sure that the fresh materials are ready for you, even if you have no notion as to what they are.

Our aim is *new knowing* with Supermind. With it, doubts disappear forever. This new knowing comes by voluntarily entering into our doubts, then passing beyond the very false ideas that caused them.

## The Grand Summary of Psychic Success

At the beginning, do not assume that you can always separate true ideas from false ones. You cannot. Do not feel badly about it, but try to understand. If you assume that you already know the difference, you fall into the trap of the conditioned mind. You will accept or reject ideas according to old, fixed standards. You may accept a false idea merely because it is novel or popular. And, you may reject a true idea because it seems strange or uncomfortable.

It is to your best interests to not look for the noisy and the spectacular on the road to the Supermind. The truth works silently but surely. If the idea comes from a spectacular person, remember that few oysters contain pearls. He is going at it all wrong and he will incorrectly lead you.

In psychic matters no authority exists outside your essential self. See the difference between acting from borrowed ideas and from the inner sense of rightness. Abandon pseudo-authority. Live from yourself. You can and must earn your own rewards. Attempts to gain unearned rewards cause damage to both the giver and the receiver.

No one, absolutely no one, has the right to judge you. You must be your own judge, but you must judge justly, thus allowing the expansion of wholeness.

If we choose the easy way, by letting another think for us, we must eventually tread the hard way. If we select the hard way, by insisting upon our own mental integrity, we eventually come to the easy way.

The path to the Supermind is plainly marked. Live with *your* thoughts, *your* feelings, *your* reactions, *your* pleasures.

We can now meet a grand summary of every true teaching ever given to man. It combines ancient wisdom with modern psychology; the technique of the East with the knowledge of the West. If you studied nothing else in this book but these principles you would have the key to the celestial kingdom:

1. *From a false sense of self arises false desires*

2. *From false desires arise false activities*

3. *From false activities arise false problems*

4. *From false problems arise false sufferings*

That this is the actual state of man cannot be doubted. No question about it, man is lost. But that is only half the story. Let's look at the bright side by reversing the process:

1. *Lose a false sense of self and lose false desires*

2. *Lose false desires and lose false activities*

3. *Lose false activities and lose false problems*

4. *Lose false problems and lose false sufferings*

In this manner man can save himself.

## General Thoughts for Specific Aid

1. It is not rough at all, once you truly understand.

2. Our frantic attempts to bring Life to our doorstep are the very things that keep it away.

3. Can you imagine what a real world it would be if no one assumed behaviors he thought he was required to have?

4. It is quite possible to observe the madness of the world without having anything to do with it.

5. No matter what your exterior activity may be, if you do it consciously, you live fully for that moment.

6. Do not lie in bed, permitting negative mental movies to run across your mind.

7. Only when you no longer know what you think is right, will you be able to effortlessly follow what is truly right.

8. Stay away from people who say they want to do things for you.

9. If we dilute the intensity of our suffering by distracting ourselves from it, we lose a rich opportunity for preventing future suffering.

10. When you know what to do with yourself when there is nothing at all to do, you have entered the golden archway.

11. Everything depends upon how far you are willing to go.

12. Whoever will go through the frightening process of abandoning his acquired human wisdom, will be carried effortlessly by Cosmic Wisdom.

13. To exchange one acquired or conditioned opinion for another is as useless as exchanging a wax apple for a plastic banana in the hope of satisfying hunger.

14. Whatever "bites" you is inside.

15. Offer no complaint to things that don't happen to you and you will know a peaceful secret unknown by millions.

16. Receptivity is an openness toward Truth while its counterfeit of shallow curiosity is openness toward negativity.

17. Trying to beautify a life based on false ideas is like placing a bouquet on a steel trap.

18. Cosmic love does not give us what we think we want, but what we truly need.

19. Be simple and you will be supreme.

20. If only you will listen, you can hear good news from yourself at this very moment.

21. A true gift, without strings attached, must come to you unasked. It cannot be pursued.

22. Nobody owes you anything at all, for the good reason that no human being has anything of true value for you.

23. Get over that secret belief of yours that you need to depend upon others for your well-being.

24. You grow healthier as you less and less hide things about yourself from yourself.

25. Your final goal is to cease to frantically think your way through life and let life think itself through you.

## Your First Three Weeks with *Supermind*

The whole human problem is lack of mental light. And so we race around in panic, like a soldier caught at night behind enemy lines. We fail to see the most obvious of facts, for example, that a man with a million dollars is not a success; he is only a man with a million dollars.

Lack of light is stubborn and self-willed refusal of light, which creates self-contradiction. A man will fiercely cling to and even praise the beliefs by which he lives, *while living miserably.* How in the world can such a man be called intelligent? Of course, his self-defeating behavior proves a familiar rule: We can't see what we won't see. And we won't see because we fear the temporary anxiety caused by seeing ourselves as we really are.

It is good news to see the origin of our distress in the wrong use of the mind. It means that correct use can correct us.

To build a glowing fire in your fireplace, you take certain actions. A match is struck to paper. You let the flickers of flame spread to wood shavings, then to the logs. You add more wood from time to time. You do not abandon effort if you fail to start the fire with your first match, nor if things move too slowly for you. You proceed with patience and persistence. Finally, the fire glows all by itself.

Likewise, you must constantly feed your inner light with esoteric ideas of the *Supermind*. This includes diligent reading, discussing things with like-minded people, observing yourself every day. After reaching a certain point, the fire glows all by itself. But this does not mean a slackening of effort; it means effort of a higher and more rewarding quality.

I encourage you to make an extra effort with *Supermind* for the first three weeks. Let these weeks mark a definite turning point in your life.

*If we would put some slight stress on ourselves at the beginning, then afterwards we should be able to do all things with ease and joy.* (Thomas á Kempis)

## Special Ideas from *Supermind*
## for Your Own Reference

In your rereading of *Supermind*, you will come across certain ideas of special meaning to you. Their value can grow for you as you nourish them with pleasant reflection. In your own words, write them down in the blank spaces provided below, noting their book pages and feel free to add pages for many more entries. In a spirit of enjoyable enthusiasm, refer to them for your own inspired guidance.

1. _____ Page _____

_____

2. _____ Page _____

_____

3. _____ Page _____

_____

4. _____ Page _____

_____

5. _____ Page _____

_____

6. _____ Page _____

_____

7. _____ Page _____

_____

8. _____ Page _____

_____

## How to Have Everything Right Through the Supermind

9. _____ Page _____

_____

10. _____ Page _____

_____

11. _____ Page _____

_____

12. _____ Page _____

_____

13. _____ Page _____

_____

14. _____ Page _____

_____

15. _____ Page _____

_____

16. _____ Page _____

_____

17. _____ Page _____

_____

18. _____ Page _____

_____

19. _____ Page _____

_____

20. _____ Page _____

# Notes

# More Notes

# About Vernon Howard

Vernon Howard was born in Haverhill, Massachusetts on March 16, 1918. When he was a boy his family moved to California where he lived for many years. He began writing and lecturing there on spiritual and psychological topics. He eventually moved from Los Angeles to Boulder City, Nevada where he lived and taught for many years. In 1979 he founded New Life Church and Literary Foundation.

From 1965 until his death in 1992 he wrote books and conducted classes which reflect a degree of skill and understanding that may be unsurpassed in modern history.

*Human Behavior Magazine* once said of him, *"Vernon Howard is probably the clearest writer on these subjects in the English language."*

His warmth and refreshing sense of humor made him a delightful subject for interviews, talk shows and articles. In 1983 Michael Benner of station KLOS in Los Angeles, California said, *"Vernon Howard is one of the most powerful speakers I have ever interviewed. He has an uncanny ability to cut through the fluff and puff and jolt people into seeing who they really are. At times humorous and gentle, at other times demanding and forceful, Vernon holds the record for generating responses to our KLOS talk shows. Not everyone likes his message, but I can't imagine anyone turning him off."*

Vernon Howard broke through to another world. He saw through the illusion of suffering and fear and loneliness. In *The Esoteric Path to a New Life* MP3 Compact Disc there is a marvelous interview with Vernon Howard. Also included in this album is the booklet of the same name, which will give any new student a great introduction to Vernon Howard's teachings.

Today more than 8 million readers worldwide enjoy his exceptionally clear and inspiring presentations of the great truths of the ages. Libraries, bookstores, health food stores and church bookshops all over the country sell Vernon Howard books, booklets, CDs, DVDs, MP3 CDs and more. His material is widely used by doctors, psychiatrists, psychologists, clergymen, counselors, educators and people from all walks of life.

All his teachings center around one grand theme: *"There is a way out of the human problem and anyone can I find it."*

## About New Life Foundation

New Life is a nonprofit organization founded by Vernon Howard in the 1970's, for the distribution and dissemination of his teachings. It is for anyone who has run out of his own answers and has said to himself, *"There has to be something else."* These teachings *are* the something else. All are encouraged to explore and apply these profound truths — they work!

The Foundation conducts classes on a regular basis throughout Arizona, Colorado and Southern California. They are an island of sanity in a confused world. The atmosphere is friendly, light and uplifting. Don't miss the opportunity to attend your first New Life class.

*For more information on books, booklets, CDs, MP3 CDs, DVDs, classes and more, call, write, fax, e-mail or visit our website at:*

## www.anewlife.org

*Headquarters*
**NEW LIFE FOUNDATION**
**PO Box 2230**
**Pine, Arizona 85544**
**(928) 476-3224**
**Fax: (928) 476-4743**
**E-mail: info@anewlife.org**

**TELL A FRIEND!**
Send us names & addresses